The Chinese Empire, Illustrated

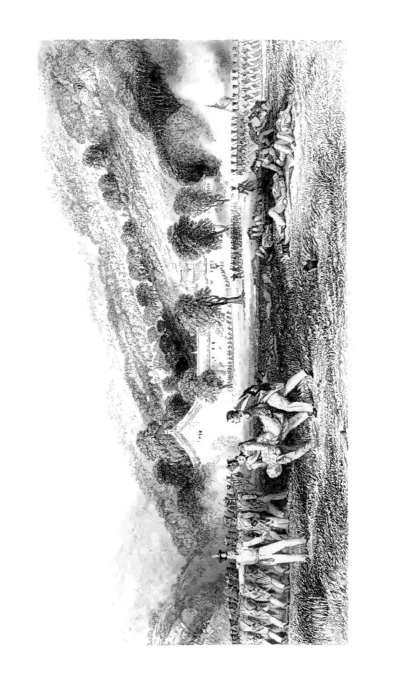

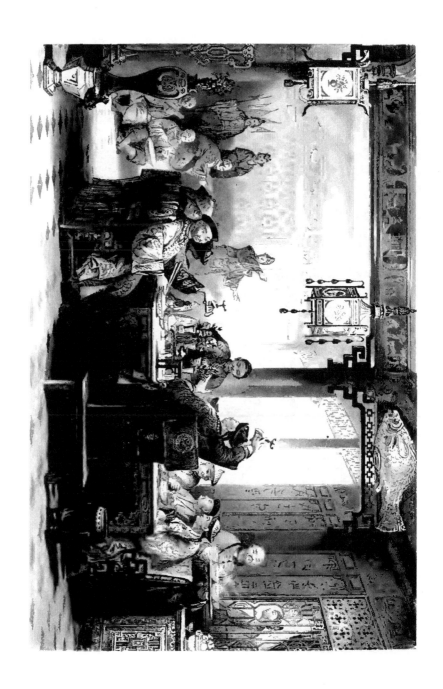

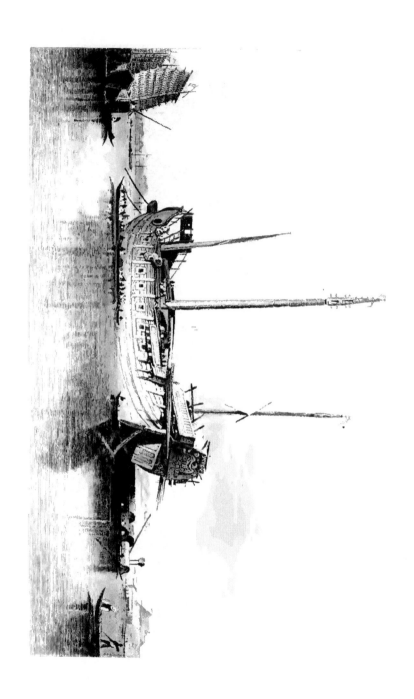

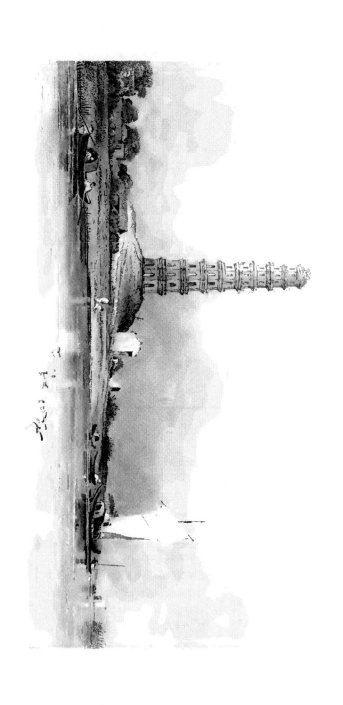

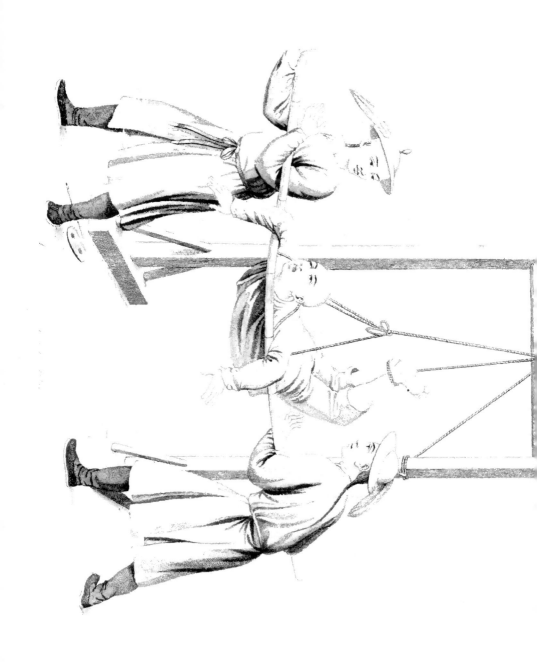

precipitous, but fertile, are adorned with the most luxuriant vegetation and foliage. the sacred temples that rise from the one, are embraced by the shade of the other, and their tapering proportions alone break the continuous mass of verdure that clothes the whole pyramid, and, descending in graceful forms, sweeps with tender sprays the waves that ripple on the beach Temples, and towers, and bonze-houses, peep forth from the embosoming woods, while a graceful pagoda, of the most exquisite structure, surmounts the highest point. Wherever civilization has established a stable tenure, there the ministers of religion appear to have selected, for the setting up of the altar and the accommodation of its servants, those retreats best suited to holy meditation, and in so doing, they have evidently paid due homage to the fairest forms and chiefest acquisitions of nature Christian monasteries are not only the most sumptuous works of art, but have been uniformly raised in the richest and most romantic districts of every enlightened land In this respect, the Chinese have not exercised less diligence, taste, and judgment, than the priesthood of Christian countries: and the picturesque circumstances of their idol-houses and dwellings, have at all times induced that class of travellers to deviate from the highway to their gaudy shrines, from which the most liberal contributions were to be expected

Richly adorned with luxuriant trees of every species known in the province of Kiang-su, the aspect of this bright isle is further broken and beautified by the most fantastic architectural forms. Here the disciples of Confucius, Laokien, and Fo, have erected temples to their respective deities, while the delicate pagoda, a feature for ages identified with Chinese landscape, lends increased dignity to the majestic form of the whole composition The double-roofed building, overshadowed by weeping branches, and standing on the margin of the river, was formerly the dwelling of Bonzes, but it is more than probable that these impostors were compelled to migrate when the emperor Kien-lung built a villa here, and laid out a moiety of the island in pleasure-grounds, disposed after the peculiar manner of landscape-gardening prevalent amongst the Chinese It was the whim of this capricious autocrat to visit occasionally the southern provinces of his vast empire, and the locality of Qua-tchow being salubrious and remarkably picturesque, was selected as suitable for the erection of an imperial lodge Near to that flourishing city, and at a place called "Woo-yuen,"or "The Five Gardens," a palace was immediately raised, which continued, with little interruption, to be the favourite retreat of majesty for many successive years. Its spacious grounds were adorned with pavilions, grouped or isolated, communicating by corridors, or other minor constructions, together with flower-beds, artificial ruins, factitious rocks, and hollowed grottoes. A meandering river, crossed by numerous bridges, and conducted ingeniously through all the intricacies of this fairy labyrinth, at one time contracted between wooded banks, at another expanded into lakes with islands floating on their glassy surfaces, completes the inconceivable illusion as to extent and intervening distances. The principle of deception so successfully matured in Chinese landscape-gardening, by which space acquires apparent extension, from an increased number of intervening objects or ideas, appears to have been borrowed from an analogous mode of measuring time adopted by philosophers, namely, the number of intervening ideas

Although the fairest formations at Woo-yuen have been effaced, and time has spared little more than the material atoms of the extraordinary designs here pictorially illustrated, one apartment is still jealously preserved, and shown to travellers with an air of pomp and mystery this is the library in which the great Kien-lung once sought rest from

" Public noise and factious strife,
And all the busy ills of life "

Here he reflected, probably, upon the best means of relieving himself from the anxious solicitude which the government of so many millions must necessarily have created—perhaps, also, upon the vanity of all worldly greatness, since one enemy remained who was invincible—and perhaps, also, upon his own individual unfitness for the great trust committed to him, and on the best and most ingenious mode of escaping from the importunities of his own conscience Amongst the many modes to which the imperial owner had recourse, to while away his leisure in the Pavilion of "The Five Gardens," poetry appears to have been included , and some few lines which he composed upon the charms of the imperial retreat, have been carved upon a slab of black marble preserved in the library, and are still shown as a specimen of his genius and penmanship, the engraving being also a fac-simile

That his time might be divided as much as possible between the fairy-grounds of the Five Gardens, and the sunlit banks of the Golden Island, the emperor Kang-hi caused a canal to be cut from his pavilion to the waters of the Yang tse-kiang, passing the flourishing city of Qua-tchow The distance of the embouchure of this still-water navigation from the shores of the Golden Island, is about two miles, yet such is the extravagance of Chinese vanity, and such the extent of their credulity, that tradition ventures to maintain " that a bridge constructed to facilitate the imperial intercourse between these favourite spots, once spanned the breadth of the Kiang's waters "

The panoramic view from the pine-clad summit of the Golden Island* is extensive and varied. It includes the mouldering walls of Qua-tchow, with its still more desolate imperial gardens; the city of Chin-keang seated at the base of a lofty mountain-range, besides the various sweeps and windings of the imperial canal and of the Yang-tse-kiang In this district white and coloured marbles, as well as sienitic granite, abound , of the latter, the bridges of the province are mostly built The principal trees are the plane, pine, cypress, arbor-vitæ, willow, camphor, and *yang-choo*, the last is a spreading tree that droops its branches to the ground, where, like the *ficus indicus*, they take root, and become each in turn a fruitful plant.

* The most celebrated amongst the many isles, or rather hills, in China, distinguished by the prefix " *Silver*," is situated to the west of the city of Chin keang foo It was anciently called " The Land of Deer ," but from its proximity to the Kin-shan, acquired its present more conformable epithet Under the Ywen, or Mongol dynasty, a temple was built upon its summit, the praises of which were sung by Lew-yen-paih, a member of the Tang dynasty, a family much celebrated for their exquisite taste in poetry

AMOY, FROM KO-LONG-SOO.

"With varied colours drest, the mountain-steep
Reflects its radiance o'er the glassy deep,
Nature's broad mirror, where its giant form
Is seen through ages, scathless mid the storm."　　H

ALTHOUGH long excluded from intercourse with this picturesque port, the English had early habits of commercial friendship with the citizens   Here a stirring and a sterling trade existed before foreigners were restricted in their barter to Canton, and none of the five free ports thrown open by the interference of British arms, welcomed back the stranger with more sincerity than that of Heamun   An island, fertile and fortified, obstructs the winds and waves in their progress from the east, rendering the inner cove always smooth and sheltered   But this agreeable spot, called by the natives Ko-long-soo, or island of crystal fountains, is insufficient to save the vessels that he inside from the depredations of desperate men, that seek their sustenance by piracy alone   All night long the hoarse sounds of "red artillery," booming heavily along the waters, tell that the crews of the junks at anchor in the bay, are prepared to defend themselves against sudden aggression, and this practice prevailed even while British men-of-war lay moored in the offing

Nothing can be imagined more pleasing, picturesque, and animated, than the prospect of this vast mercantile harbour from the heights of Ko-long-soo. The deep channel, crowded with junks, is at the observer's feet, the narrow promontory forming a chief suburb, projects beyond   further still is the second passage, backed by those noble hills of granite which separate the marine district from the mainland. The entire scene has a magical effect

ANCIENT TOMBS, AMOY.

"Perhaps in this neglected spot is laid
Some heart once pregnant with *celestial* fire,
Hands that the rod of empire might have sway'd,
Or waked to ecstasy the living lyre "　　GRAY's *Elegy*

EVERY addition made to our knowledge of Chinese history and habits, contributes to render the analogy with other Oriental countries closer, by which their vain notions, of a separate origin from the rest of mankind, meet with circumstantial contradiction. Ceremonies in honour of the dead, form no minor criterion of previous identity, and, whenever we find two nations, or people, observing rites nearly similar, and those of a very complicated character, it may, with great probability, be concluded, that they are derived

from a common origin   All the forms of a Chinese marriage are discoverable in some
country or other of the Eastern hemisphere, their affectation of peculiarities being an
insufficient disguise   So also, in the burial of the dead, a striking similarity to the practices
of countries described in Scripture, has been ascertained, by modern travellers, to prevail
in China. Exploring parties of British officers, actuated by no other motives than those of
curiosity, amusement, or instruction, set out from Amoy, and, ascending the granite hills
that shelter and adorn the vicinity, were astonished by the discovery of an ancient
cemetery   It occupied a hollow or excavation in the mountain, such as would have
been left by an extensively wrought quarry, and, from its weather-worn appearance,
was evidently of most ancient construction. A crescented tomb of triple walls, dedicated to a mandarin of high rank, stood in front of the enclosure, behind which rose a long
flight of steps cut in the rock, leading up to a gateway of grotesque design, consisting of
a double ogee-roof, sustained by four wooden columns   The inner space had evidently,
in former ages been excavated, the stone carried away, and the regular area left by its
removal, formed into galleries and promenades, rising in tiers one above the other   In some
instances, vast spaces were enclosed by walls of solid masonry, within which were temples,
or tombs, hollowed from the rock, and filled with remains of the dead. In other
directions several hundred vaults stood, with opened doors, upon a gallery of considerable
length   In some cells, urns, in others coffins, were found, while many had become
altogether deserted and tenantless   Here however, incontrovertible evidence is offered,
that the Chinese anciently—for these sepulchres are by themselves, considered to rank
amongst their earliest records of civilization—entombed their dead in catacombs, like many
other Oriental nations   The Egyptians constructed pyramids and labyrinths, to contain
the remains of mortality   The Phœnicians and Greeks hollowed out rocks for tombs,
surrounding their chief cities with depositories of the bones of their fathers   Beneath
Rome, Naples and Paris, are extensive catacombs: and gigantic constructions of a similar
description, but far more early dates, exist on the African shores of the Mediterranean
The doors or the panels cut in the rock on each side of them, in these catacombs of Amoy,
are carved with appropriate inscriptions, and with effigies of wives or attendants, or slaves,
or horses, or other objects that contributed to the honour or happiness of the deceased
This custom is precisely co-incident with that of the most ancient Egyptians   There
the catacombs give us an idea of those whose existence is still unknown to us   They contain the history of the country, and the customs and manners of the people, painted or
sculptured in many monuments, are in the most admirable preservation

It was customary in China to bury slaves and even queens, alive, with the remains of
emperors and princes, but, the Tartars substituted the less cruel and sinful system of
burning representations of all imperial attachés in tinfoil, and of placing little wooden
images of them also upon the graves of their royal masters   The former custom, according to Herodotus, prevailed amongst the Scythians   at the funerals of their chiefs
wives, servants, and horses were all impaled alive, and placed around the tyrant's tomb
In Egypt, the hieroglyphics on the walls of the mausoleum express the extent
of the deceased prince's authority, the number of his slaves, and of his subjects,—at

Amoy, the devices on the rocks are intended to express similar objects. These tombs, therefore, only made known to Europeans since the return of our victorious expedition from China in the year 1844, afford a convincing proof that the primæval habits of the Chinese did not differ from those of the earliest people spoken of in the Scriptures, for they also placed their dead in grottos.

It may give confirmation to the conclusion here attempted to be drawn, to quote this well-known passage in the sixth Æneid of Virgil.

> Those pleasing cares the heroes felt, alive,
> For chariots, steeds, and arms in death survive,

as evidence that the Romans were familiar with that kind of sepulchral sculpture, which perpetuated the dignity of the deceased hero · and a passage in the Electra of Euripides,

> Thou *Queen Earth*, to whom I stretch my hands,

demonstrates an analogy between the funeral rites of the Chinese and the Greeks, all tombs in the kingdom of Cathay being, to the present day, consecrated most especially to *How-too*, or, "queen earth."

CITY OF AMOY, FROM THE TOMBS.

> "A city pleases me. I have intense
> Delight in human effort, and my soul
> Becomes as 'twere a portion of the whole,
> In all its beauty and magnificence." MARY HOWITT

CAPTAIN STODDART'S accurate view of the site and scenery of this celebrated entrepôt, is a panorama of exquisite loveliness. Employing the ancient burial-ground as an observatory, the eye ranges over the low-lying city with its embattled walls; the wide-spread suburbs, with their countless cottages, beyond these, again to the land-locked cove, dotted with busy merchantmen there riding securely from every breath of wind. Above the waters of the inner bay, which closely resembles an inland lake, rises a noble chain of mountains, dentated in outline, and granitic in structure. Ko-long-soo, interposed between the outward ocean and this picturesque basin, acts as a natural and most efficient breakwater, imparting such entire and constant placidity to its surface, that vessels may lie here at all seasons regardless of the weather, biding their time for unfurling the sails, and transit from shore to shore by the smallest boats, is never attended with risk or interruption.

Being nearer to Canton than the other open ports of the empire, Amoy will probably be sooner, as well as more securely, enriched, by the abolition of commercial monopoly at that much-disliked emporium, and we may expect that European intercourse with the port will be greatly increased by recent events

THE FORTRESS OF TERROR, TING-HAI

"Go standard of England, go forth to the battle,
Go, meet the proud foes in their hostile array,
The heat of the action where loud cannons rattle,
Is where I have borne thee through many a day."
                        The Soldier's Farewell to his Flag

Now HERE, during the British descent upon the coast of China, was the destruction of life and property greater than at Ting-hai.* Situated in the entrance to the bay of Hang-tchow-foo, Chusan might operate as a breakwater against the ocean's waves, a fortress against foreign wars; but in the latter capacity it proved lamentably deficient. In the first volume of these descriptions, the fall of Ting-hai is recorded, almost in the language of an eye-witness; it is preceded by a brief, but faithful, description of the port and city, to which we refer the reader. It is remarkable that those places which the Chinese government believed to be impregnable, yielded readily to British arms, while positions of less reputation afforded more obstinate resistance. Every hill on the coast in the vicinity of Ting-hai, is crowned with a battery of apparent strength, some too elevated to be effective, others too much exposed to the fire of an enemy. At the entrance of a defile, watered by a rivulet flowing from the valley of Chae-hu, and on an eminence about two hundred feet above the level of the bay, stands one of those deceptive structures, misnamed "The Fortress of Terror," in which the Chinese so lucklessly reposed entire confidence, when the British fleet cast anchor in the roads beneath.

No troops, however armed or disciplined, could have acted with more eminent personal gallantry, than the Tartar garrison of the fort of Terror, yet none ever encountered a more signal overthrow. Two circumstances contributed to produce this result; one, the scientific principles, perfect discipline, and national courage of the British; the other, ignorance on the part of the Chinese, of all modern improvements in the destructive art of war. Hereafter these hill-forts may be strengthened, and rendered serviceable, yet even this hope would appear to be extinguished by the extensive application of steam in the British navy.

In one of the picturesque and rocky glens of Chusan, and immediately behind the city of Ting-hai, where several spacious villas are erected, stands a grotesque-looking Hall of Ancestors,—octagonal in form, and covered with a lotus-shaped roof, having dragoned finials; it is open beneath, and, from its pleasant position on an elevated rock overhanging the glen, and commanding a prospect of the fortress in front, and of the sea at its base, is a constant scene of visitation. In Chusan, generally, there are many indications of a very ancient occupation, perhaps none more obvious and useful than the old paved roads

* *Vide* Vol I, p 75]

leading up every glen, and often climbing to the summits of the hills, the best examples of these may be seen in Anstruther's Valley, and at Pih-chuau One well known paved-way, crossing an artificial river by a wooden bridge, ascends the ridge of rock on which the open temple rests, and, descending on the other side, passes the lower walls of the fort, and continues to Ting-hai Although a mandarin of some consequence, as his retinue implies, is seen approaching the temple in his sedan of ceremony, the roads of Chusan were not constructed for the convenience of visitors, the gratification of travellers, or the mere objects of pleasure Every hill is cultivated to its summit, every valley, from the mountain's foot to the river's margin, and, as industry and fertility are here happily concomitant, a large surplus arises for the enrichment of the labourers These productions, including rice, cotton, sweet potatoes, coarse tea, and candles made from the seeds of the tallow-tree, are conveyed along the canals in barges, and afterwards carried to the sea-ports by the usual mode of transport in China, the bamboo-pole laid across the shoulders, with buckets, or baskets, or boxes suspended from its extremities. In the agreeable scene, with which the faithful pencil of Captain Stoddart has made the western world familiar, little boats are just arriving at a convenient place for landing or receiving burdens, and, beyond the pool, a picture still more animated presents itself, in the bustle of the boatmen and porters belonging to a large farm-house, the paddy grounds of which are supposed to lie behind This pleasing spectacle is singularly characteristic of Chusan landscapes, everywhere in this cheerful island, hills and valleys, woods and rivers, luxuriance and sterility, are seen in contrast, and, the precise beau-ideal of romantic beauty amongst Chinamen,—the end so eternally pursued in their landscape-gardening, namely, the introduction of rocky-groups, and forest-trees, and running waters, amidst the highest state of refinement and cultivation, is effected in Chusan, by a generous co-operation of nature

---

GRAND TEMPLE AT POO-TOO,

CHUSAN.

No regal state with eating cares intrude
To break the stillness of his solitude,
No wealth allures, with all its glittering store,
But peace, contentment, wait the bonze's door.   H

Poo-Too, or Worshippers' Island, in Chusan archipelago, is the chief seat of Chinese Buddhism, and has long been celebrated for the riches, and magnitude, and glories of its temples. Although the whole area of this sacred spot does not exceed twelve square miles, nor its original population two thousand souls, yet here now upwards of 3,000 monks, or bonzes, of the Hoshang or unmarried sect, reside, and lead a Pythagorean life Three hundred isles and upwards, constitute the Chusan group, many of which are larger and more fertile than Poo-too,* but none comparable to it for inequality of surface, variety of scenery, and boldness of outline when seen from a distance,—shelter and repose when closely visited For the latter reasons, doubtless, these ascetics selected the deep glens of Poo-too for their temples, and for their tombs. Upwards of four hundred minor chapels have been erected on this little isle, but there is one building which is considered the very cathedral of Buddhism. In a fertile and narrow valley, overhung by gigantic summits that reach, in some places, to a height of one thousand feet, and traversed by a rivulet of clear, sweet water, stands The Grand Temple. Between two tall flagstaffs, planted securely in the natural rock, a flight of steps ascends to the simple gateway leading to the court, monastic dwellings, of two stories in height, substantially built, and surmounted by hideous dragons, are grouped closely together, and behind them rises the many-storied pagoda, that marks the site of the temple of worship It is more than probable, from the solitude and study to which the bonzes of Poo-too dedicate themselves, that they are acquainted with the labours of the Catholic missionaries who once visited their country, and who were so favourably received by Kang-he It is also perfectly certain that they are familiar with the mode of worship observed by the Portuguese at Macao, because crucifixes and images of our Saviour, and of the Virgin Mary, mixed with articles of a general character, are publicly offered for sale in the shops of Ting-hai These notorious facts will therefore explain the anomalous appearance of a large and well-carved cross, conspicuously placed on a sculptured and solid pedestal, being found amongst the external architectural decorations of a Buddhist temple

Although Buddhism is a religion confined to its officiating priests, the public feel an interest in its preservation, as communicating to social life a moral impulse They contribute, therefore, alms to the priests, and donations to the pagodas When Nanking was restored, after its devastation by the Tartars, the green and yellow tiles of the imperial palace, in that city, were presented to the bonzes of Poo-too, and, being placed on the great temple, they now reflect the bright rays of a mid-day sun, with a brilliancy that is observable many miles from the Island Quan-gin is the most revered idol in the grand pagoda, but Teen-how, or the Queen of Heaven, is enthroned in the smaller ones. In all of them are colossal images of Buddha, either in a standing or sitting posture, and, in some instances, surrounded by upwards of fifty of his disciples, fashioned from clay or plaster In the chief saloon of the great temple, a large and beautiful bell, sculptured with inscriptions, and scalloped at the mouth, is preserved, and, beside it, rests a drum, the head of which is about eight feet in diameter, covered with ox-hide

* Trading-junks uniformly call here on their outward passage, and the crews get their fortunes told For a small sum they obtain an amulet, or charm, which is deemed a certain preventive to shipwreck, and a secure guarantee of a prosperous voyage

THE BRIDGE OF NANKING.

"Have not those ancient arches stood,
Time out of mind, the angry flood ?
What busy crowds have paced their length,
Safe in their firm and long-tried strength "

Ghost of London Bridge

IT has been previously stated in the pages of these volumes, that Nanking is not seated immediately on the banks of the Yang-tse-kiang, but at the distance of three miles from them, and connected with that noble river by a wide and deep canal, so considerable, indeed, is this artificial navigation, which continues parallel to the west and south walls of the city, at a trifling interval only, that the bridges thrown across it are works of much architectural pretensions Near where the Porcelain Tower formerly stood, the largest and principal bridge of Nanking spans the main trunk of the canal, forming a communication between an extensive suburb, and the west gate of the city It consists of six well-turned arches of unequal width, and is altogether a scientific work, being kept down nearly to a level with the banks at either extremity.

Chinese bridges are constructed on different principles, in different parts of the empire, so much indeed does diversity prevail, that is, science in one place, ignorance in another, that neither censure nor applause can be bestowed upon the architects of the empire generally in this particular respect. Arches, pointed like the Early English, may be found in one locality, the horse-shoe, or Moorish form, abounds in another ornamental bridges, in gardens and pleasure-grounds, consist mostly of one opening, either arched or flat; some of those built over navigable rivers have piers so lofty, that junks of two hundred tons burden can sail under them without striking their masts, one arch, and of large dimensions, is of frequent occurrence, so also are bridges of a number of arches, and that near Sou-tchoo-foo consists of no fewer than ninety-one

That beauty and strength are not inseparable in works of art, is at least fully illustrated in the structure of the graceful one-arch bridge of China. Each stone is cut so as to form the segment of a circle, and, as there is no keystone, ribs of wood, fitted to the convexity of the arch, are bolted through the stones by iron bars, fastened securely into the dead-work of the bridge Sometimes wood is dispensed with, in which case the curved stones are mortised into long transverse blocks of the same material. In some parts of the empire, on the other hand, arches of smaller stones, and pointed to a centre, as in Europe, are everywhere seen. The arches of the towers on the Great Wall, are all exactly turned, and the masonry of that miracle of labour is referred to by those who have examined it, as a perfect model of enduring industry

From what has here been stated, it would appear, that not only are the Chinese in perfect possession of the true scientific principles of arching in masonry, but still fur-

ther, that they acquired that knowledge before any other known nation   Arches cut
in the solid mountain occur in Hindoo excavated temples, but, when independent stones
were employed, and the building was to be superstructed on columns, then the stones
above the capitals were overlaid, like inverted steps, till they met in the central point
above and between the two columns, resembling, at a little distance, a Gothic
arch   Neither the Persians nor the Egyptians appear to have been acquainted with
the circular arch, for no such form occurs in the runs of Persepolis, Balbec, Palmyra,
or Thebes, nor does it seem to have been much used in the magnificent buildings of the
Romans, antecedently to the time of Augustus   Those that are now disclosed in the
disinterred fragments of Pompeii, are on a diminutive scale, seldom employed to sustain
a heavy weight, but principally to decorate and relieve the monotony of a continuous
surface   If Chinese annals deserve any credit, the arches in the towers of the Great
Wall were constructed before the western nations of the world were acquainted with the
invention   But, independently of their own testimony, circumstantial evidence favours
the decision, that, with them, this discovery of so much beauty and utility, first
originated

The bridge of Nanking is built entirely of red granite, with circular arches turned
with cuneiformed stones, and resting on piers of solid masonry   That its projectors
were little apprehensive for its stability, is shown by the erection on each side of the cause-
way, of a row of substantial dwellings, one story in height   These do not prove as
injurious as droves of cattle, coaches driven at a rapid pace, or armies marching with
regulated step (the most severe test of a swinging bridge), but they do, to a certain
extent, establish the sustaining ability of the structure.   On one side of Nanking great
bridge is shown the city wall, on the other the once famous Porcelain Tower, while the
state-junk, conveying an imperial commissioner, who had just arrived to treat with the
English, has reached its berth at the principal landing-place.

FOOT OF THE TOO-HING, OR TWO PEAKS, LE NAI.

PROVINCE OF CHEN-SI.

> "'Tis good to climb the mountain high
> And trace the valley deep,
> To gaze upon a brilliant sky
> Where clouds of silver sleep "   ARGYRO CASTRO

FEW scenes in the whole empire of the Chinese, more fully illustrate the jealous policy
of its government than the picturesque locality of the "Two Peaks"   Not deeming this
rocky barrier sufficient protection against the untamed animals, rational and irrational,
of the desert, the Great Wall has been continued on the other side of the mountains of
Chen-si, without sufficient reflection, by its royal founder, upon the ridicule so super-
fluous a defence might probably excite   Against all such apprehensions, however, the

legislators of China appear to have been completely proof—remaining eternally wrapped up in ideas of the antiquity, majesty, populousness, and power of their country. Nor is this more than useless wall, raised to defend the Too-hing, the only act of conspicuous folly and bigoted policy which the vicinity discloses. Valuable mines of gold lie buried in the rocky treasury of these mountains, easily accessible to such skilful miners as the Chinese, but they are prohibited from being worked, on pain of death So resolute on this point is the imperial decision, that a guard of tiger-hearted Tartars is stationed at " Two Peaks," to prevent the least attempt at seeking for this source of human weal and woe

A high road, from the Oilous country to Sin-gan-foo, through the Too-hing mountains, was formed, it is said, some thousand years since, and by upwards of one hundred thousand labourers. High hills were levelled, deep valleys filled up, and bridges thrown across chasms, and ravines, and defiles, from mountain to mountain In some places roads were conveyed on pillars, like our grand modern aqueducts of Europe, across low districts of miles in length, in others, as at " Two Peaks," a passage was cut through the solid rock, and, with an expenditure of manual labour never known but in China, steps hewn in a lofty mountain from its base to its summit. At the commencement of this zig-zag avenue a guard is stationed, under the command of officers having authority to exact toll from passengers and duty on merchandise. A station-house at the upper gate is of singular construction. The passage hewn in the rock being only wide enough to admit a sedan, with a foot-passage at a side doorway,—the guards are lodged in a series of apartments elevated on poles some twenty feet above the road Besides transit duties, a very considerable amount of revenue is derived from the productions of the district itself. The climate is suited to the cultivation of rhubarb, honey, cinnabar, musk, wax, and odoriferous woods of the sandal kind. Although the inhabitants are not allowed to touch the gold, they raise coal in great quantities, besides several species of minerals employed by native physicians as remedies for fever, and as antidotes against poison Stags, fallow-deer, wild oxen, and fierce animals of the feline species, range these rocky regions their capture affording constant employment to the natives, and their skins constituting a source of wealth. In the low districts, where the river periodically inundates the land, wheat and millet are raised in abundance, but little or no rice

This perhaps is too commercial, too utilitarian a picture, of this remote but romantic locality, nor is it in all respects a full and fair one, for, in addition to the varied forms of the Too-hing summits, the luxuriant vegetation of intermediate valleys, and salubrious quality of the climate, no province of China is more richly adorned with instructive examples of natural history. This is the country of that beautiful spotted animal resembling the leopard, for which a name is yet wanting in English, of the Chinese chamois, from which musk is obtained, of The Golden Hen, the pride of the feathered tribe, in Asia, and, here also, amidst a myriad of blushing companions, *The Queen of Flowers* has established her superiority More delicately coloured than the rose, its leaves are larger, its perfume sweeter, and its blossoms endure much longer.

WEST GATE OF CHING-KEANG-FOO.

Now came that awful conflict big with fate
The band, in order, in their barges sate
By sounding oars, and sinewy arms impelled
Their course, to reach that field of war they held
ARGON EXPED

WHERE the Imperial Canal enters the Yang-tse-kiang river on the south, and where a broad and beautiful nautical basin is formed by the river's sinuosities and expansions, a vast trade has been contracted, and large cities have grown up. In the centre of the river, at its widest part, stands the Golden Island, clothed to its tapering summit with the most luxuriant foliage, on the northern shore is seated the city of Quang-tchou, and, on the southern Ching-keang-foo. Ridge after ridge of rocky mountains stretches away from the borders of the bay into the remotest distance, producing a remarkable contrast of imagined retirement and sterility, with the smiling and animated picture which the river, here a league in breadth, presents to the eye. The surface is varied by the presence of vessels, differing in size, shape, and objects. Some sailing with, others against the current, many crossing from one adit of the canal to the opposite, and countless numbers lying at anchor.

Ching-keang-foo being the key to the southern provinces, the out-port on which Nanking depends for its security against foreign aggression, was deemed of corresponding importance to the British troops in the subjugation of the Chinese empire. Being strongly protected by walls, thirty feet in height, and five in thickness, containing a large and active population, and being garrisoned by a body of resolute Tartars, its reduction was considered both the more necessary and more glorious to our army. Ascending the canal, and effecting a safe landing on both sides of the water, at the foot of a lofty and noble bridge of one arch, the British commenced a vigorous assault upon the west gate of the city. A much warmer reception than was anticipated, at first threw the assailants into some confusion, and the Blonde's boats, after a desperate resistance, were actually for a while in the enemy's hands. From this perilous position, however, they were soon released, by a party of marines and seamen belonging to the Cornwallis.

This momentary discomfiture only lent new resolution to those who were its victims, and, under cover of a destructive fire from the opposite bank of the canal, Captain Richardson led up a scaling party to the walls. Rockets and heavy guns soon overthrew the gate-towers, and the gates themselves becoming a mass of flame, destroyed all prospect of future resistance. Submission now was the sole remaining alternative for the Tartars, who had fought with courage and devotion.

Only four miles in circuit, Ching-keang-foo is but a minor city, indeed it is the fifth in magnitude in Kiang-nan however, from its geographical position, it is always esteemed one of the first in commercial rank The streets are narrow, paved with marble, and contain many well-supplied shops.

NANKING,

AS IT WAS SEEN FROM THE PORCELAIN TOWER

"There is a majesty more felt than seen,
In the vast city with its peopled homes,
And hearts all full of an immortal life,
Thousands and tens of thousands beating there "
CONSTANTINOPLE

THE form of the enclosure, or *enceinte*, of ancient Nanking is very irregular, having been accommodated to the inequalities of surface and limits of inundations that occasionally take place In one part lofty hills arise, affording a prospect over the whole urban and suburban area, in another the dwellings are brought into close and constant contact At the south-west angle, where the public offices are placed, and a water-gate leads to a spacious four-arched bridge, that crosses the canal, is that suburb situated on which the famous tower looked down for so many centuries. It was destroyed by the Taiping rebels in 1856 With the disregard for antique remains such disorderly bands frequently exhibit, they blew up the fine edifice, which had so long been the boast of China, and only its ruins now remain * Eastward, is still seen the Tartar keep, an *imperium in imperio*, city within city, being securely enclosed by its own walls, although in the very centre of the great fortified area itself Beyond and northward, lofty, steep, and sterile hills, some included within the mural cincture, rivalled the pagoda in towering height. Farther still, continuously, the Yang-tse-kiang, like an inland sea, expands its broad surface to the mountain's foot, and at some three miles' distance, is the junction of the canal of Nanking with that great and noble river Some distance from what was the base of the Porcelain Tower, is a courtyard of oblong form, having at its further extremity a hall of learning or of religion, according to circumstances, and on either side are cells, appropriated to the idle bonzes, who live in tolerable ease on public generosity Large tracts of uncultivated land appear to be the property of this inactive community, but whether they disdain labour, while they are not ashamed to beg, or some religious scruple intervenes, these appear devoted to eternal sterility. From this bird's-eye view of Nanking, a correct idea may be formed of the social architecture of the Chinese, and the systematic arrangement of their civic avenues Discipline, method, established obedience, are conspicuous in every part,

* A description of the Porcelain Tower, as it appeared previous to 1856, will be found in vol 1, p 162

and when the populousness of the empire is considered, the statesman may possibly find reason to conclude, that the freedom of the subject has not been unnecessarily coerced, nor the administration of justice neglected, in this ancient and absolute despotism

It was at the influx of the canal of Nanking, the north-west corner of the city, that the British vessels of war, Cornwallis and Blonde, cast anchor, with orders to effect a breach in the walls, which catastrophe the astonished citizens averted by a timely submission. This point was visible in the panorama as it was witnessed from the tower, as well as the extremity of the paved road, seven miles in length, leading from the gate of victory to a landing-place, on the Yang-tse-kiang, near to which the transports were directed to anchor on the same occasion The imaginative portion on the right of the accompanying view, is the *enceinte* of the ancient city,—on the left, the remainder of the town-suburb *

SILVER ISLAND,

ON THE YANG-TSE-KEANG

These Islands that, empurpled bright,
Floated amid the livelier light,
And mountains, that like giants stand
To sentinel th' enchanted land
The Island

WITHIN view of the Golden Island, and on the bright bosom of that wide expanse of waters westward of Chin-keang-foo, the Yin-shan, or Silver Island, rises with much beauty and grandeur, from the surface, less lofty and precipitous, less adorned also with pagodas and palaces, than its more favoured rival, Silver Island is nevertheless possessed of features both pleasing and picturesque The richest foliage clothes its sides and summit, cottages and villas peep forth from the dense masses of deep verdure that conceal its form, and, from the great depth of water close to shore, the scene is uniformly enriched by the accompaniment of large barges and trading-junks at anchor all around, their forms being distinctly relieved upon the verdant surface behind them The fleet of Queen Victoria having anchored close to these isles of beauty, and a strong detachment having been landed at Ching-keang-foo, Chinese infatuation was from that moment dissipated The stranger had found a highway to the best cities in the bosom of the empire, and social intercourse with foreigners had always been considered, by Chinese rulers, as an experiment too dangerous to be tried. No sooner, therefore, had an easy victory crowned with success the British arms, than the government prudently resolved upon submitting to whatever conditions the conquerors thought it expe-

* *Vide* further details of Nanking, in vol 1, p 116, and of the Porcelain Tower, p 162

dient to propose The capture of the Golden and Silver Islands, the occupation of the wide expanse of waters that encircle them, by a British force, decided the contest between England and the Chinese empire

It is about six hundred years ago, since a Temple to Fo was erected here, and a Hall of Learning attached to it ; and so great was its sanctity at that period, or shortly after, that the praise of its priests, and the natural beauties of their rocky domain, became the theme of Lew-van's most celebrated songs This prince and poet first employs the more ancient name Keen-too-shan, or hill of solid earth, in his poems, but subsequently, in speaking of the comparative beauties of the sister isles, introduces the epithets Yin-shan and Kin-shan.

An enthusiast who once dwelt here, in the temple founded under the Yuan dynasty, pretended to powers never committed to the control of erring mortality. He professed to render the persons of his consulters proof against the point of the dagger—the flame of the fire—the strain of the rack This avocation was successful in filling his treasury, the victims of his imposture, probably, being unwilling to acknowledge how completely they had been duped But, just when he imagined his throne to be established, the emperor, who had been informed of his guilt put him to death by that cruel process called " Ling-chy," or cutting into ten thousand pieces.

DICE-PLAYERS, NEAR AMOY.

He knows his fault, he feels, he views,
Detesting what he most pursues ;
His judgment tells him, all his gains
For fleeting joys, are lasting pains

The Gamester

The Abbe Grosier says, " the Chinese are entirely ignorant of all games of chance " so far is this from being true, that there is no nation in the world, the humbler classes of which are so entirely the slaves of this besetting vice To this hateful propensity is to be ascribed their indifference to manly exercises, and to all those nobler sports that impart health and vigour to the body, generosity to the mind They practise fishing less as an amusement than a trade, employing in its pursuit an endless number of snares ; such as the varnished plank facing the moon; the flat and the purse nets, dulls and gins of various kinds, three-pronged spears, the bow and arrow, and the diving cormorant. Hunting is held in little estimation, the farmer being at liberty to save his crops by destroying all those animals that are deemed destructive to vegetation. While fishing, fowling, and hunting, are thus excluded from their national amusements,— theatres, kite-flying, cricket and quail-fighting, lot-drawing, mora-playing, cards and dice, prevail universally.

The picturesque spot on which Mr. Allom has spread a bamboo mat, for the idle Haimenese to indulge their morbid taste, is in the solemn locality of the city of the dead,—the ancient tombs hewn in the solid rock, records which the very gamblers, who desecrate the scene, hold in the utmost veneration

The encouragement of this demoralizing vice by the Chinese, creates a distinction peculiarly remarkable, between that nation and the ancient kingdoms of Europe In the latter, so far back as we have historic information of the fact, gamblers and spendthrifts were not only held in utter detestation, but punished also by public marks of degradation and contempt Seneca calls the fruits of gaming, "the baits, not the boons of fortune," another wise man pronounces the catastrophe of such a life to be sorrow, shame, and poverty By an edict of the emperor Adrian, gamblers were declared to be prodigal fools, deserving of public reprobation, and exclusion from all societies The Beotians brought their ruined spendthrifts into the market-place, an empty purse being carried before them, and, placing them on a stone called the prodigal's chair, left them exposed to the scoffs of the multitude Near to the senate-house, in Padua, may yet be seen "the stone of turpitude," devoted originally to a similar purpose, and, some early European civilians thought that guardians might be appointed to save the property, and observe the actions, of a gambler, in the same manner as well-ordered governments, in modern times, protect the persons and estates of all acknowledged lunatics

---

ENTRANCE TO THE CHIN-CHEW RIVER.

FOKIEN

Though the grave were in his way,
Forward, would the Briton say,
And upon his latest breath,
Would be " Victory or Death "

IN its progress northward, after Amoy had been captured, the British fleet entered the estuary of the Chin-chew river, on the south bank of which, but some miles inland, the city of Tscuen-tcheou-foo is situated As this port was the very focus of the contraband traffic in opium, some rude preparations had been made to resist the approach of a hostile expedition Description of those puerile operations is superseded by the intelligible, and very clever drawings of the scene, which the portfolio of Captain Stoddart, a sharer of the expedition, placed under Mr Allom's control The Chinese junks kept at a respectful distance, from the boats of the detachment that was ordered to effect a landing at the foot of a bluff on the north side of the river, and, as to the brave Tartars, who were placed there to serve the guns on shore, after a few discharges only, they fled in the wildest dismay, abandoning their copper ordnance and all their ammunition to the enemy   The material of which they were made, rendered the captured cannon something more than trophies of glory   the value of those taken at Chin-hae alone, exceeded £10,000 sterling, and the spoils of Woo-sung were still more important.

The commercial city, to which the Chin-chew river is the highway, holds a distinguished place amongst those of the first class   inferior to few in geographical position, and in healthful trade, it is eminently adorned with triumphal arches, temples, and other public edifices, its streets being remarkable for their extent and width   Seven cities of the third rank are placed under the protection of this ancient and populous foil   It is in the immediate vicinity of Tsuen-tcheou that the extraordinary bridge is to be seen, which Martini has described in the following terms,—" I saw it twice, and each time with astonishment   It is built entirely of a blackish stone, and has no arches, but upwards of three hundred large stone pillars, which terminate on each side in an acute angle, to break the violence of the current with great facility   Five stones of equal size, laid transversely from one pillar to another, form the breadth of the bridge, each of which, according to the measurement I made in walking, was eighteen of my ordinary steps in length, there are one thousand of them, all of the same size and figure. a wonderful work, when one considers the great number of these heavy stones, and the manner in which they are supported between the pillars   On each side there are buttresses or props, constructed of the same kind of stone, on the tops of which are placed lions on pedestals, and other ornaments of a similar description." Many lives having been lost while ferry-boats were the only means of crossing these troubled waters, a certain humane governor of the city constructed this splendid monument to his fame, at his sole expense   That expense, if reliance may be placed on the accounts of the learned Du Halde, amounted to half a million sterling.

CHINESE BOATMAN ECONOMIZING TIME AND LABOUR.

P O O - K E O U.

"Now he weighs time even to the utmost grain."—HENRY V

On the north bank of the Yang-tse-keang, and opposite to the canal that extends from that river to the walls of Nanking, may still be seen the mouldering battlements of Poo-keou-hien   These primitive defences were never of considerable height or strength, and their preservation is less to be ascribed to original solidity, than to the mildness of climate and conservative disposition of the native population   The enceinte of the deserted city is now grown over with shrubs and wild flowers, and such is Chinese veneration for ancient places—so great the superstition that protects all records of days long numbered—that not the slightest trespass is ever committed upon this solitary site. Nature has resumed her empire within the walls which the industry of man had raised for her exclusion.   The forsaken pagoda that crowns the summit of a rocky eminence, rising rather rapidly above the river, consists of five stories, resting on a substructure, that would appear, from the solid quality of the natural foundation, to have been altogether unnecessary. From its plain decorations, and very inferior style, it may probably have been dedicated to the winds, or the waves, rather than to Buddha, whose priests would not readily have abandoned a position so agreeably and felicitously placed for the visits of votaries   In several places of China, known to Europeans, temples of the winds have been found, without either priests or protectors, and resigned, like the forsaken pagoda of Poo-keou, to the mercy of their tutelar deities.

Its proximity to Nanking gives ample employment to the rural population of this district, and facility of water-conveyance is amongst the chief advantages which they enjoy   'Tis true, labour is cheap where hands are numerous, and the Chinese are more lavish of manual workmanship than any other people that we are acquainted with , yet in some few instances they seem to practise an economy in time and trouble, totally at variance with their habitual extravagance of both, in all others   A market-gardener of Poo-keou, having loaded his boat heavily with fruit and vegetables, erects a bamboo mast, unfurls a sail of bamboo-fibres, and, drawing together the bamboo cords that constitute his reefing-tackle, makes fast their common extremity to a pin beside him Placing his pipe securely in his mouth. and his broad bamboo hat as firmly on his head, he proceeds upon his voyage ·—should the wind be sufficient to fill his sail, then with one hand he tightens or relaxes his tackle, and with the other holds the helm   One oar is allowed to lie idle, but the other is worked advantageously, both for guidance and propulsion, with the foot   This illustration of customs forms a striking contrast to another, which the same scenic representation exhibits   While the economist of labour is passing in his laden boat, fishermen are actively engaged with their trained diving-birds, procuring a supply for the market of Nanking   In this most tedious process, the sagacity of the cormorant is alone entitled to our admiration , the indefatigable patience, that caused its development, deserving little more than our compassion.

THE VALLEY OF CHUSAN.

"The uplands sloping deck the mountain's side,
    Woods over woods in gay theatric pride,
    While oft some temple's mouldering tops between,
    With memorable grandeur mark the scene "   GOLDSMITH

THIS beautiful panorama displays the majestic character of the scenery amongst the Chusan group with the best effect and the most entire truth   It presents all the happy combinations of mountain, water, wood, waste, and cultivated lands, that occur in the landscapes of this archipelago , and although detached from the continental territories of the empire, Chusan is in every respect a true evidence of the cultivated condition to which the Chinese people have attained by their long and undisturbed repose. Nowhere could a scene be found more fully developing climate, agriculture, and national habits than the accompanying comprehensive view. The climate is of a medium temperament between Peking and Canton, and life, accompanied by temperance, is, at Chusan, usually prolonged to many years.

ARRIVAL OF MARRIAGE-PRESENTS AT THE BRIDAL RESIDENCE.

" And God that all this world hath ywrought,
Send him his Love that hath her so deere bought "

CHAUCER

WHENEVER Providence has distinguished the bride from the bridegroom by rank, wealth, or other adventitious circumstances, the marriage contract in China too nearly resembles a bargain for sale and purchase. It may unquestionably be retorted, that the practice of setting a price on female loveliness degrades the social customs of European life, and that both wives and husbands are occasionally purchased in the most civilized kingdoms of Europe, yet, in all such cases, there is one redeeming virtue not found in Chinese ethics, namely, that the principal parties to the contract, the lovers themselves, have the privilege of a previous acquaintance. Should report celebrate the charms of a lady amongst the higher classes in the Celestial empire, purchasers soon appear, to solicit her hand,* and, so soon as the monetary arrangements are concluded, the suitor is permitted to send rich presents to his lady-love In this act of courtesy, this subscription to custom, he is joined by his relatives and private friends, who vie with each other in making offerings, costly in proportion to the dower to be received with the bride, or paid to her parents   These gifts are to be carefully distinguished from the coarser specimens of art borne in the marriage-procession. They consist of trinkets and toilet-furniture, silks and silver-ware, and the manner of their presentation is peculiarly ceremonious. One of the chief apartments of the house is allotted to the reception of such tokens of respect: there the female heralds are admitted, and acknowledged with some degree of solemnity, while around are seated in sorrow either serious or assumed, the sisters and and near kindred of the bride   To the elder ladies of the family belongs the duty of laying out the gifts judiciously in the inner chamber, the bride meanwhile, in her broidered cap, occupying a conspicuous place, and expressing her thanks to the various messengers of kindness

The late professor Kidd observed a remarkable analogy between marriage ceremonies amongst the higher orders in several Oriental kingdoms, but especially the Malays and

* *Vide* vol 1, p 134

Chinese   " Theie were three days of feasting and pieliminaiy amusements, duiing which the bride was visited by hei friends, and adorned by hei attendants with jewels, raiment, and peifumes, supposed most likely to render her acceptable to the bridegroom On the evening of the third day fiom the commencement of these ceiemonies, when the biide was shut up in her own apaitment, with hei female friends, the bridegroom came to the dooi, and demanded admission   A voice fiom within asked who was theie ? and on what eiiand the visitoi had come ? questions which the bridegroom answered by calling aloud his name, and demanding the young lady within to be given to him as his wife In reply, he was desired to state what present he pioposed to make, if the doors were opened ? A diamond of consideiable value was promised.   The door was imme-diately thrown open, and the husband, on piesenting the precious gem, was admitted to the piesence of his bride , who accompanied him to the nuptial feast spiead upon a mat on the flooi, on which they both sat down to eat   It was at the feast, piepared in the evening, and consisting of all the delicacies afforded by the climate and the season, with a large bowl of rice in the centie, that the ratification of the marriage agreement took place, which in its essential points is the same as among the Chinese , and was in all probability the primitive custom of sanctioning mairiage   It is impossible, in iefeiring to those obseivances, not to be struck with the illustrations they affoid of customs and expiessions in the Sacred Sciiptuies, such as decking the bed of the biide of Solomon anointing the person of the bride with peifumes and myrrh,—the great gaiety and fes-tivities of the paity, kept up for a considerable peiiod, accoiding to the iank of the individuals, and various other points of coincidence."*

ANCIENT BRIDGE, CHAPOO

"Bridges, and palaces, and towers,
Now rise by such strange quick'ning powers,
That we, who come of ancient race,
Must travel with a slower pace "   H.

In piimitive forests, where time and tempest stiuggle for dominion, huge trees aie prostiated by these giant poweis, and thiown into singulai positions.   Sometimes they fall and lean against each othei, in a Gothic arch, sometimes they lie in heaps, like basaltic columns, and at otheis they stretch acioss the ravine oi the torrent, as secuiely as if science had lent her aid in their disposition   It was such accident, if there be chance in the operations of natuie, that first suggested the idea of the horizontal bridge, consisting of a single plank , hence it may with some probability be concluded, that the flat aich is the most ancient in use, not only amongst the Chinese but other nations also   At later periods, when industry and civilisation had giown old together, these people executed works of the gieatest engineering difficulties , amongst such are biidges of some huudred arches, resting on pieis of solid masonry, triumphal monuments of the richest design, arches, and aqueducts.   Even the art of tunnelling was eaily practised,

* Vide China, by Samuel Kidd , p 325

and it is several centuries since Colao, a native of Quang-tong, caused the high moun-tain that hangs over Nanking to be pierced through from north to south, by a high road for travellers

The flat bridge of a single opening on the river of Chapoo is obviously of the most early style Strong abutments being constructed, large flags are laid, lapping one over the other like stairs, to the edge, or nearly, of the pier, from which flag-stones of requi-site dimensions are laid across the interval In the next era of bridge-building the Egyptian arch was adopted, in the third, the segment of a perfect circle

On the balustrade of Chapoo bridge, lions couchant, rather rudely executed, are placed, emblematic of the magnificence of the structure, or the great ability of the architect. In no country is learning held in higher esteem, art pursued with greater zeal, or genius more uniformly rewarded The captain of a Tartar band, who succeeds in annihilating or dispersing a banditti, is honoured with a triumphal arch, on which his exploits are blazoned in letters of gold; temples are raised to the shade of the philosopher; and the fame of the artist is perpetuated by various types of national eulogy. The engineer of the great tunnel at Nanking is ever before the eyes and the minds of his country-men, a monument to his honour being placed on the highest pinnacle of the mountain which the tunnel pierces The memory of their princes is also preserved by architec-tural testimonials, inferior, however, in most instances, to the monuments of those whom science or virtue has rendered illustrious Although women are secluded from public life in China, they are treated with the utmost tenderness, their lords pretend-ing, that it is solely with a view to spare their feelings, that they do not require them to participate in the active duties of society. Whether this be a specimen of Chinese duplicity, or a true and genuine sentiment, it is certain that the highest honours are frequently paid to female virtue, and the praises of the softer sex are not only cele-brated in the stanzas of the poet, but obelisks and arches, and monuments of the most costly character, are also raised, to mark a nation's admiration of the high qualities that distinguish mother, wife, and daughter

ATTACK AND CAPTURE OF CHUENPEE.

"The trench is dug, the cannon's breath
Wings the far hissing globe of death
Fast whirl the fragments from the wall,
Which crumbles with the pond rous ball,
And from that wall the foe replies,
O'er dusky dales and smoky skies "   BYRON

THE principal entrance of the Pearl river is between Chuenpee and Tycocktow forts, the outer defences of that great emporium, the city of Canton   To the west is an extensive delta, intersected by numerous branches, all, however, too shallow for any other than flat-bottomed craft   but with these a considerable trade is carried on between Canton and Macao.   During the opium war, the English commanders, through the effrontery and arrogance of Commissioner Lin, were compelled to attack and capture Chuenpee   The accompanying plate represents that achievement, of which an account will be given in the history of that war, in subsequent pages.

PAGODA AND VILLAGE ON THE CANAL,

NEAR CANTON

"Here on a clear and crystal bed,
A sparkling radiance round thee shed,
Thou view'st the forms and shapes that rise,—
Spires—villages—delight thine eyes "   H

ANIMATION increases as the city of Canton is approached, not solely from the cultivated character of the enclosing banks, or the constant passing of vessels engaged in foreign trade, but more particularly from the vast amount of population permanently located on the watery surface   Pilot-houses, stores, merchants' villas, and groups of humble dwellings, overshadowed by waving pines, lend an air of cheerfulness to the ever-varying view, and the style of architecture, combined with the seasonable decorations of the houses, add much agreeable effect to the moving picture   One locality is peculiarly gratifying from the liveliness of the scene, and assemblage of pleasing objects and circumstances   A row of picturesque cottages, on one bank, is approached from the water by a broad flight of steps, shaded in hot weather by the outspread branches of a lofty forest tree, on the opposite bank stands a temple of Fo, and a tall pagoda encircled by ramparts, where the Chinese sustained, for some twenty minutes, an attack from a small British force in the recent war with the empire   It is at this place, called the Yellow Pagoda, that so many junks stop, and their crews, disembarking, make offerings to the tutelar deity of the islet for their safe return, or conciliate his favour for a prosperous voyage   From this venerated spot to the city quays, activity, and indeed confusion, appear to increase with an accelerated speed, so that when once the noble panorama of the Yellow Pagoda, the majestic stream of the Cho-keang, and the distant amphitheatre of hills are passed, Honan and the sounds of the city streets are soon encountered.   This is the principal suburb allotted to foreigners for their residence, but the privilege is accompanied by so many infringements, that the value of the gift is much less than the giver could ever have contemplated.   Every promenade is previously occupied by the most idle and ill-conducted of the native population, intermixed with a countless crowd of beggars   These troublesome characters hitherto, that is, previously to the Chinese war, with unblushing effrontery gathered around each foreigner, either to satiate vulgar curiosity, or extort, by pressing importunity, undue alms.

Beyond, or rather through, a dense forest of masts, a view is obtained, from this suburb, of the European pavilion at Canton, and of the factories, as they existed previous to the close of 1856   approach, however, appears to be difficult.   Barges, barques, boats, junks, and larger vessels lie side by side in one continuous arrangement on the surface, and there is no avenue for a new arrival.   The custom-house, therefore, could not be reached without the aid of a constabulary force.   Even with these auxiliaries the achievement was one of considerable difficulty—one in which torrents of abusive language were sure to flow, repeated blows being often interchanged, and personal injury not unfrequently inflicted   Some abatement from the uniform violence of these scenes took place subsequently to the opening of Ning-po, and of other ports, the establishment of more free traffic at Macao, and the settlement of Hong-Kong by the English, but the Cantonese retained an extensive foreign trade; the population of their city kept increasing; and they were not without the hope, that the exclusive system might be again revived, and restore to them their much-abused monopoly of European and Indian commerce   a hope which must now be considered as doomed to complete disappointment

---

SCENE ON THE HONAN CANAL,

NEAR CANTON.

" And here the wide earth's treasure
Shall merchants bring—spices, and gems, and gold;
All precious wares for pride, and pomp, and pleasure,
Shall here be bought and sold "   MARY HOWITT.

Not far from the celebrated temple* is the embouchure of the Honan Canal, a principal highway of traffic, and an avenue to scenes of beauty, industry, and cultivation.   Villas erected at immense cost line the banks in many places, their balconies being decked with fragrant flowers, adorned with fantastic lanterns, and distinguished by various other productions of an ancient refinement   Like the palaces of Venice, each villa has a separate

* *Vide* vol 1 , p. 142.

cove, or fairy port, where the barge of its wealthy owner lies moored, until the sounds of pleasure once more call it into service. In some places the store, or factory, of a merchant stands on the margin of the water, a broad ladder descending from the lowest verandah, for the convenient delivery or reception of merchandise, while tablets hanging from the pillars indicate the name, and quality, and particular business of the proprietor. Those who have made a tour of the Venetian lagunes, are prepared to appreciate the pleasant character of such watery ways, where familiarity soon obliterates the idea of danger, and novelty insensibly adds zest to enjoyment. Immediately above the locality represented in Mr Allom's view, is a bridge of unequalled grandeur—the proud architectural boast of the Cantonese. Here the Fan-kwei has always been allowed the privilege of mixing with the subjects of the celestial empire, gazing on their singular costume, their splendid parasols, and their inexpressive countenances, while he is himself, in turn, the object of an unenviable examination. On this grand rialto fortune-tellers and begging bonzes make their stations. The former either move amongst the passing crowd, or seat themselves at a table, on which writing materials are laid, and, for a few *cash*, unfold the mysteries of time to come. Husbands who have forfeited their wives' affections, lovers who would ensure the regard of their Dulcineas, mothers who burn with solicitude for their children's happiness, and children who have been discarded by their parents, these, and other varieties of suitors, are seen around the magician's table, awaiting, in breathless eagerness, his sentence, or their turn for consultation.

Above and below this favourite promenade the scenery of the canal is remarkably picturesque. The character of the architecture, the species of foliage, and the sleepy surface of the liquid way itself, are similar all along for many a mile, but nowhere so strikingly beautiful and agreeable as in the immediate vicinity of Ta-jin's pavilion. The principal front is sustained and decorated by colonnades so light, and delicate, that a breath would appear sufficient to blow them away, yet so solid and secure, being formed of bamboo, that they are competent to resist the rudest visitations of weather. Colours the most bright, smiling, and gaudy enliven the upper stories, from the gilded lattices of which the females observe all passengers, without being themselves discovered by the objects of their curiosity.

As your boat is pulled leisurely along, you may peep into the interior, and witness the glowing reign of luxury. There a multitude of sparkling lustres, twinkling lamps, and glaring lanterns depend from the ceiling, while everything that can minister to social enjoyment is spread around these grand saloons. Let the eye but turn to the opposite shore, and dwell upon the contrast in place and circumstances · there riches are succeeded by poverty—leisure by industry—perhaps also affectation by real happiness. Fronting the villa of the prince-merchant of Honan, is the poor-man's hut, built on piles that out-top the water, and beside it is a narrow space, overshadowed by the branches of a full-grown tree, where all his commercial negociations are conducted. Here the poor but civilized Chinaman, with a species of practical philosophy, peculiar to countries where the necessaries of life are few in number and easily obtained, leads a kind of nomade existence. His embowered wharf is equally adapted to the transactions of trade and the pleadings of pleasure , and thus he whiles away one day after another, regardless of what the following may require

But the Chinese, or rather Cantonese, population do not restrict their residences to land, nor to houses resting on piles near the shore, multitudes have their homes upon the deep, for they actually dwell in barges moored in the river, and never abandon that amphibious locality for the safer land   In some parts of the river the number of fixed barges is so great, as to conceal the greater portion of the channel's breadth, and present a solid jumbled mass. In others they are arranged with their sides contiguous, and extending from shore to shore, with the exception of a narrow passage for the shipping Groups are often detached from the land and moored in tiers, admitting of communication amongst themselves, but preventing intercourse with the shore. This aquatic race of human beings is viewed by their brethren of the *terra firma* with suspicion and unkindness   They are believed to have had a separate origin—considered as aliens of contemptible talents, and prohibited from intermarrying with lands-people.   Tradition, most foolish tradition, ascribes their origin to the wide-spread space beyond the embouchure of the Choo-keang, an idea as childish as the fable of mermen, or sons of the sea. It is to the grandfather of Teaou-kwang that the water-population of China are indebted, not only for being admitted to citizenship, but even for permission to set foot on the soil of the celestial empire

----

JOSS-HOUSE, CHAPOO.

DEATH OF COL TOMLINSON

"Whatever heavens, sea and land begat,
Hills, seas, and rivers, God was this and that "   Jer

THE fall of Chapoo and death of Colonel Tomlinson have been described in the pages of our preceding volume,† the accompanying view places before the reader the local characters of the scene on which it occurred

In other countries, as well as in China, temples of religious worship have been converted into places of temporary defence, in time of war, and garrisoned by gallant companies that have done honour to their country   Instances are so numerous, that no student of history can be unacquainted with some of them   The positions of churches, either on a conspicuous eminence, or in a sheltered glen—either in the very centre of the village, or commanding its entrance—having a tower well suited for a military post, from which musketry can act, with dreadful effect, upon an assailing party, render their occupancy always a point of importance.   And it may accordingly be

* For further particulars of the river population of China, *see* Introduction to vol 1 , p x.
† *Vide* vol 1 , p 126

observed, that the most fatal encounters, in every aggressive war, have arisen from a struggle for their possession * The death of Colonel Tomlinson was attended with circumstances of greater gallantry than any other event in the Chinese war, and the obstinate defence of the Joss-house at Chapoo may be appealed to by the Tartars, as an evidence of their personal bravery.

Like the religions of the Chinese, their places of worship are also various. temples, on an extensive scale, capacious and lofty ; but joss-houses, of minor proportions the former often adorned with pagodas—the latter seldom , but, both possessing accommodation for resident bonzes, and altars for consultation, to which votaries bring joss-sticks, and perfumes, and tin-foil, and other ingredients requisite for the performance of ceremonies calculated to propitiate the tutelar deities How these inferior gods became entitled to this worship is probably little understood by the frequenters of their temples, especially since the number is considerable, and the idea attached to the divinity of many somewhat complex Besides Halls of Confucius, Joss-Houses, or Halls of Ancestors, Temples to Buddha and Taou-tze, there are *Miaos* to the Mother of Heaven, the God of Fire, the Devil Star, the Four Chaste Ladies, the Dragon King, Literature, the Winds, Longevity—deities who attend travellers, and conduct them home in safety; and others, of whose offices the description would be still more tedious To all these objects of worship, joss-houses appear to be consecrated, and to some of them, (the *du majores*, probably,) greater buildings. Notwithstanding the obvious folly of the Chinese modes of worship, there is one principle connected with them that is exemplary —toleration Nor is the objection of much weight which ascribes that quality to indifference rather than liberality, for, the Chinese may employ the arguments of Symmachus, a bitter enemy of Christianity, who yet maintained the free exercise of conscience in matters of religion " Because God is immense and infinite," says this epistolary author, "and his nature cannot be perfectly known, it is convenient he should be as diversely worshipped as every man shall perceive or understand "—a deplorable theory, yet the offspring of reason The same writer recommends, " that every province should retain its own institutions, revelations, orders, oracles, which the genii of the place may, from time to time, have dictated to their priests or ministers." There cannot be a more accurate account of the plurality of religions that prevail in China, nor of the grounds on which toleration is permitted in that empire.

* In the late war with Russia, several monasteries in the White Sea were fortified, and became the objects of hostile attack from the importance of their position

A TARTAR OF THE CHINESE ARMY.

"In spite of bitter thoughts, and angry words,
One hundred spades are worth one thousand swords"

VARIOUS accounts have been published of the Chinese army,—of which, in fact, till within the last few years, very little was known * A recent French writer estimates its number at 900,000, Tartars and Chinese Mr Keith Mackenzie, in his "Narrative of the Second Campaign in China," informs us, that the entire Tartar force is "divided into eight divisions, distinguished by the colour of their respective flags, the yellow, or imperial colour, being the highest. Next are the white, red, and blue banners, the other four standards are formed by one of these flags, bordered by another colour Each Tartar standard has 10,000 Tartar soldiers attached to it A green flag is used by the Chinese soldiers only ; and all yellow flags have the imperial yellow dragon worked in the centre "

The fighting-men of the Chinese army are, undoubtedly, the Tartars, who are really soldiers by profession There are horse and foot and in the north of China large bodies of the Tartar cavalry are still armed only with swords, and bows and arrows, the latter being a much more useful weapon than the cumbrous and uncertain matchlock of the Chinese, though greatly inferior to the old "Brown Bess," and falling infinitely behind the Minié or Enfield rifle of the modern English soldier The infantry number archers in their ranks , they also use the matchlock, the spear, the pike, and the scimitar , they wear the latter on the left side, drawing it by putting the hand behind the back , as, were they to draw it from the front, it would expose the arm to an adversary. The matchlock, as we learn from Mr. Keith Mackenzie, is, as nearly as possible, the old European weapon of the same name; but, subsequently to the peace of Nanking, Ki-in, who signed the treaty of 1842, and Mon-tchang-ha, the Chinese prime minister, or president of the council, exchanged, to a certain extent, both bow and arrow and matchlock for the percussion gun The spears and pikes are of all kinds, sizes, and shapes, the favourite pattern being a long broad blade. The British found them, in the "opium war," capable of inflicting "most horrid wounds " Some of the Tartar infantry use a peculiar kind of cross-bow, which we have already described,† and they are very expert in its use The bows and arrows are alike, whether borne by mandarin or private , the only difference being in the material. The quiver of the soldier is lashed tight on the back , and, for the convenience of carriage, is generally square

Mr Keith Mackenzie describes the uniform of the Tartar soldiers as "very much a

---

* Some particulars relative to this army will be found in the articles on the "Military Station at Cho-kien," pp 11—44, and "The Emperor Toon-kwang reviewing his Guards," pp 143, 144, vol 1

† Vol 1 , p 43

mattel of fancy, the jackets being generally made of a light blue cloth, tuined up with red, or else a red jacket, bordered with white, the tunic, or under-garment, reaching down to the knees, and being generally blue." But the Russian traveller, Timbowski, who visited a large part of the Chinese empire, states, that the soldiers are "clothed the same as the other inhabitants, with the exception of the tunic, which they wear over all, it is always of the same colour as that of the flag under which they serve,—that is to say, yellow, white, red, or blue, with or without border. In times of war," he adds, "they receive helmets of iron, cuirasses that are quilted and wadded, and shields of bamboo wicker-work." In 1840, the English found at Chusan, cotton dresses for the body, lined with pieces of iron plate, and also helmets of polished steel, very much resembling those worn in Europe during the middle ages. "I was not informed," says Mr. Mackenzie, "whether the use of these was confined to the mandarins, or whether the soldiers were also provided with them."

The pay of the Tartar soldier "is two taels per month, or about fivepence per day, with an allowance of rice," being nearly double the pay of the Chinese. "The reasons for this difference may be the following —First, that the Tartar in China belongs to a standing army, at a distance from his home, and is dependent solely on his profession. Secondly, some allowance may be made for the national partiality of the governing power, and the necessity of attaching its confidential servants by liberality."*

Our engraving represents a Tartar soldier—one in command—as he usually appears when on duty.

THE TIGER GUARD.

"To see their rude pastime,
When stretched out afar,—
'The Army of Heaven'!
And the 'Tigers of War'!"

The Tartar soldiers form the garrison of towns, and they are, in an especial manner, the guards of the emperor. In each town they are under a general, who is independent of the officer who commands outside the walls. He has two adjutants attached to his command they are called *Too-tung*, and one is denominated "right," the other "left," from their taking command of the left and right wings of the army. The general himself is named *Tseang-keun*, he has the head of a tiger embroidered on his outward dress, and wears a peacock's feather, with three eyes. This officer is always a member of the provincial council, and frequently acts independently of the civic authorities.

At Peking, there are eight divisions of Tartar troops, each under its peculiar-

* Davies

coloured banner   These are—1 The vanguard, picked from the Mantchoo and
Mongol troops, under eight commanders. 2 A body of infantry, or armed police,
under a commander and two lieutenant-generals   3 A body of artillery, under
Mantchoo and Mongol commanders   4 A body of scalers, under the same command
5 A troop of pioneers. 6 A troop of lancers. 7. A troop of falconers. 8 A troop
of wrestlers and archers.*   In times of peace, the services of all these troops are
confined to Peking, and, in other towns, the Tartar soldiers execute no duties beyond
the walls, except when foreign war or domestic rebellion call for their services

The "life-guards" of the emperor are called "tiger-soldiers."   They wear a striped
dress of black and yellow, resembling the tiger's skin, and close caps with two ears
projecting, as seen in our engraving   The caps are formed of split bamboo, "so com-
pactly interwoven, as to be capable of resisting a violent blow"   The shield is made of
the same material, and has the head of a tiger or of some other fierce animal, or a terrible
image, painted upon it   The duty of these guards is, to attend the emperor, and to
protect him from all enemies

The highest military post in China is that of the *Tseang-keun*   It cannot be filled
by a Chinese, indeed, it is the rule, that officers of one nation must not command the
troops of the other.   Neither Tartars nor Chinese display any knowledge of military
strategics   and that several hill tribes, even in the interior of the country, should have
maintained their independence to the present day, shows the real weakness of the
military resources of the empire   "One very singular feature we must not forget to
notice, in regard to the military officers of China.   They are all subject to corporal
punishment, and very often experience it, together with the punishment of the *cangue*,
or movable pillory †   This parental allotment of a certain quantum of flagellation and
personal exposure is, occasionally, the fate of the highest officers, and, upon the whole,
must be regarded as a very odd way of improving their military character "‡

Military colonies, somewhat resembling those of ancient Rome, have been formed in
China   They originated with the emperor who built the Great Wall, but, under him,
they were mere military posts, established to check the incursions of bands of pillagers
Finding them eminently useful for that purpose, the number of colonists was increased,
and other colonies were formed, not only on the frontiers, but in the interior of the
empire, where agriculture had been neglected.   They are of two classes—those intended
for the defence of the frontiers against invasion, and those established, in Mongolia
and the Eastern provinces, for purposes partly political and partly strategical.   Several
of these colonies were formed between 1736 and 1820, and they are all flourishing
The military colonies are part of the imperial domain   When established, every officer
and man—from the general downwards—has a plot of ground given to him, which
he cultivates at his own cost, appropriating the produce to the support of his family,
and to defraying the expenses of the colony. A colonist cannot sell his land, or
bequeath it at his death, but when the latter event happens, the emperor disposes of it.

* Martin's "China"   † See vol 1, p 173   ‡ Davies.

In 1812, the colonies were estimated to cover 4,420,000 acres, at present (1858) they extend over 7,500,000 acres They have increased, and are increasing, under the present emperor; who loses no opportunity of planting soldiers upon the uncultivated and unproductive parts of his territory

---

THE ARCHER

" All made of Spanish yew, their bows were wond'rous strong,
    They not an arrow drew, but was a cloth-yard long
    Of archery they had the very perfect craft,
    With broad arrow, or butt, or prick, or roving shaft
    At marks full forty score, they us'd to prick and rove,
    Yet higher than the breast for compass never strove "

So wrote the old poet, Drayton, of Robin Hood and his merry men—traditions of whose deeds yet abound in the neighbourhood of Sherwood Forest In their days, the cross-bow was the English national weapon, and it continued to be so till the introduction of artillery and matchlock guns, consequent upon the discovery of gunpowder, when the bowmen of England, as a part of the national army, became gradually extinct, though archery is still cultivated, and, no doubt, always will be, as an agreeable and graceful amusement

As we have stated already, the bow continues in use, in China, as a military weapon; and, in our engraving is seen the *vraisemblance* of a bold Chinese archer, smiling with perfect complacency on all around him Amongst that nation, archery has, from the remotest times, been always held in high estimation, and to be a good bowman was the great object of the majority of the male population of the empire But archery is now, we are informed, beginning to be "looked upon rather as an elegant accomplishment for gentlemen and military men—like fencing among some Europeans—than as a measure of defence or offence in actual warfare," recent hostilities having shown the superiority of the European fire-arm, in warfare, to the bow Shooting well with the bow on horseback, is still, however, regarded as a high achievement in archery, and some of the Chinese books on tactics give very precise descriptions for the acquirement of skill in this part of the art, whether it is resorted to for the purposes of war, or merely for amusement

The Rev W C Milne, who was, for many years, a missionary amongst the Chinese, thus describes a review of archers, at which he was present, in 1843 —

"Only two minutes' walk from my habitat, there was a parade-ground for military exercises Ascertaining that the horse-archers were out, I hastened to the spot immediately after breakfast The ground occupied was, perhaps, 200 yards long by 50 broad The officers present were of an inferior grade (ensigns and sergeants), except the military judge, who was seated under a canvas canopy The archers were drawn up two deep, and called out in companies of eight men, to receive orders on their knees. They then went onward to the spot marked off, one after the other mounting his steed, setting it at full gallop, and firing his arrows As each man shot off his handful, he returned, and, kneeling before his superior, received his reprimand, or instructions, or approval The bull's-eye, about sixty yards off from the canopy, was represented by three red balls, painted one above the other, upon a square sedge mat, nailed to a bamboo frame. The aim was to hit any of the balls, especially the centre one, while the horse was racing along the course. Some proved bad shots, others good, and every successful shot was announced by drum-beating "

As our former remarks* upon the Chinese army have reference chiefly to the Tartar part of it, we will here introduce a few particulars relative to the national branch of the military force of the vast empire of China

The character of a people, it has been remarked, may be judged of from their amusements. If so, the Chinese should be a military people, and very fond of war; for, on the Chinese stage, by far the most attractive spectacles are those which relate to battles, and the mock combats of the actors meet with the most enthusiastic applause But fond as the Chinese may be of mimic, they cut no great figure in real war. In ancient times, we are told, they called their soldiers " flying dragons," and " scudding clouds." In our own days, they rather resemble the latter than the former; for though they have a Chinese word equivalent to our epithet " brave" (from whence the term " *braves*"), stamped on their jackets, they are more famous for " scudding" from the field, than for showing the fierceness usually attributed to the fabulous animal But if not very fond of fighting, the Chinese like the military profession. So far from there being any necessity to enrol soldiers by compulsion, or bounty money, leave to enter the army is eagerly sought after as a favour, and as an addition to the man's means of livelihood

The Chinese soldiers are, in fact, little more than a militia, or armed police. Since the fall of the Ming dynasty, A D. 1545, the Tartar troops have been chiefly engaged in suppressing the constantly-recurring domestic insurrections; and also in the occasional " little wars" that have taken place with the Meao-tse—a hill tribe, who, though living in the midst of China, have always preserved their independence. The military duties of the Chinese soldiers, we are informed, have been almost entirely restricted to periodical gatherings, when they underwent a species of training, and were inspected and reviewed by their commanders Their field-days consisted in tumultuous and disorderly marches in the train of their mandarins, or in sham fights, conducted (as were their theatrical performances) with the din of gongs, and other noisy instruments This was united with the practice of the bow and the sword. " Reviews" occasionally took place, which consisted, principally, " in the examination of their matchlocks, their swords, and arrows, and, when they had any, of their helmets or padded armour." They make great demonstrations when training, " tearing and stamping in their exercise," as one writer describes it Besides these stated periods for discipline, occasionally the Chinese " braves" are employed to aid the civil magistrates as policemen, to act as custom-house officers at the military stations, along the roads, rivers, and canals, and also to

* See pages 75 and 76 of the present volume.

mount guard at the city gates A periodical writer says, that, " in show and appear-ance, they resemble the valiant supernumeraries who represent, in provincial theatres, the armies of Richard or Rolla Their helmets are made of paper, their boots of a coarse satin, and their uniform consists of a wadded gown and a quilted petticoat Instead of a military salute, they acknowledge the presence of an officer by falling on their knees, and, in warm weather, they ply their fans as assiduously as any dowager-duchess in an opera-box in July "*

Their dress appears to vary in different parts of the empire, for another author tells us, that " the uniform of a Chinese soldier consists of large, coarse, blue nankeen trowsers, and a red tunic with white facings " A third says—they clothe and arm themselves after their own fashion, and " their dress is usually that of the people in general, except that they have the words 'brave' and 'robust' painted or stitched upon the backs of their jackets, and 'valour' in front, they wear, also, a peculiar cap " Their pay is 4d per day, and they have no allowance of rice, as the Tartar soldiers have   " To every body of troops a certain number of standard-bearers is attached, whose duty it is to carry the colours, and wave them but no feeling of honour seems to actuate the Chinese soldier with regard to his colours, for, in the rout, down they go, and *sauve qui peut* is the cry "†

A few words as to the Chinese artillery.

The Chinese have known the use of cannon for more than 200 years, as there is authentic mention of the casting of cannon by the Jesuits, in 1636, at the request of the emperor, when the empire was threatened by the Mantchoos And, in the first attack on Canton, the landing party, which was sent on shore after the English had opened their fire, found, in one of the forts upon the river, from which the garrison had been expelled, a battery of six bronze pieces of artillery, of the calibre of 16 lbs, which were stamped, near the touch-hole, with the imperial cipher, surrounded with Chinese characters and arabesques, in the midst of which was a cross, in relief, and, below the cross, the date of 1697 Investigation proved that these cannon had been made during the time of the Emperor Hong Hi, who, born in 1653, died in 1723, and in whose reign Père Bosino, a Jesuit, superintended the cannon-foundry at Nanking   But, though cannon have been so long in use, no improvement appears to have been made in their construction, and the Chinese do not know how to use them with effect They make their guns, both for land-service and for the war-junks, of enormous weight, in comparison to their calibre; notwithstanding which, they frequently burst Some guns, captured in the second campaign of the opium war, though only 42-pounders, weighed seven tons The carriages are so constructed, that they can neither alter the direction nor the elevation of their guns, but are obliged to fire them off point-blank they have very little knowledge of engineering. Their fortifications are of enormous thickness, but, from the want of a firm cement, they are not strong They use a hand-grenade and rockets in their defence, but the latter are perfectly contemptible Some of the

* " Westminster Review "   † " Narrative of the Second Campaign in China "

artillerymen are, however, very expert in the use of a sling, from which they project a stone, with a good force and a tolerable aim.

The military of the empire are superintended by the Court of *Ping-poo*, or "Military Tribunal," or "Tribunal of Arms," at Peking Through this court all orders to both army and navy are issued, commissions granted, levies made; magazines, garrisons, towns, and fortresses, kept in repair and supplied, and the soldiers furnished with arms The orders of this superior court are carried out by four inferior ones, for different parts of the empire

---

POLICEMAN AND PRISONER

"This is your charge   you shall bid any man stand,   you are to comprehend any vagrom man in the prince's name"

IN all countries the occupation of policemen is pretty much the same—to preserve the peace and to apprehend offenders. The members of the police-force are numerous in China; and, as already stated,* the Chinese soldiers are little better than an armed police The policemen, not enrolled in the military ranks, are described by one, who according to Mr. Montgomery Martin, "has closely studied the subject," as being "a collection of the very scum of the nation; well versed in all tricks, personally acquainted with thieves, robbers, and gamblers, initiated in all the mysteries of iniquity, and often partaking largely not only of the bribes, but also in the practice of abomination, in the very haunts of vice " · Their pay is small—from one to two dollars per month; but many serve gratuitously, and some even pay for the appointment—a "proof that their situations must be worth something," for in China, any more than in other countries, men are not disposed to pay money for that which will produce nothing. Mr. Montgomery Martin himself, who is personally acquainted with China, says, that the police enable the mandarins to know everything that passes in their jurisdiction, and hence criminals are easily discovered : but their susceptibility to a bribe frequently frustrates the ends of justice.

In Peking, where the Chinese infantry form part of the police, "they keep a very strict surveillance, and are constantly in the streets, with swords at their sides, and whips in their hands, ready to strike any one who would create a confusion They take care to have the streets kept clean, and will put their hands to cleaning them themselves in case of necessity They keep watch during the night, and allow no one to go through the streets, except with lanterns, and then only on very urgent business, such as to call a physician, &c "† At Canton, the police is described as being "vigilant and very efficient." There are different grades, acting in the same capacities as our constables, thief-takers, and gaolers, these constitute the regular police; but many localities, as well as private individuals, engage their own police, who keep up a

* See *ante*, p 79.   † M. Martin.

constant nocturnal watch   Every street in the city is closed at night, and by the gates of most of them there is a guard-house, where offenders are lodged   In the winter months, when there is danger not only from thieves, but fire, watch-towers are carried up, by the means of bamboo poles, high above the tops of the houses—thus a double watch is constituted   The alarm of either "fire" or "thieves" quickly spreads from one extremity of the city to the other, and when offenders are captured, punishment is sure and summary   "The meat is on the chopping block," say the Chinese, when they see a man in the hands of the police   In minor cases, a man is arrested, tried, sentenced, flogged, and at liberty to pursue his reckless course again in less than an hour   If crowds assemble in the streets, and show the least disposition to riot they are speedily dispersed by the use of the bamboo or whip

When mandarins pass along the streets, they are preceded by police to clear the way, who call on the people to "retire" as they advance   Then follow one or more gong-bearers, whose mode of striking the instrument denotes their master's grade and office, then come chain and bamboo-bearers, immediately preceding the sedan in which the great man is borne to his destination   Servants, bearing umbrellas, pipes, and card-cases, run on each side of the sedan, and the secretaries follow.*   When any members of the crowd prove refractory, and will not move out of the way, or even if they are not sufficiently nimble in decamping, a chain is thrown over the head of the offender, and he is immediately dragged off by the police

---

EXAMINATION OF A PRISONER.

"Man, proud man,
Dressed in a little brief authority,
Plays such fantastic tricks before high heaven,
As make e'en angels weep "

The Chinese are not, as a nation, distinguished by the commission of flagrant crimes, or gross and daring violations of the laws   Still there are many offenders amongst them, and against some offences the laws are very strict, and the punishments awarded for their commission are extremely severe   The mandarins are the magistrates, and preside in the courts of justice   These courts are all furnished with a drum, which is beat by those who demand justice, to the great astonishment of Europeans   There does not appear to be any fixed period for the courts to sit, and many cases are heard by the magistrates as soon as the offender is apprehended.

The forms of justice are few and simple   When the police apprehend a Chinese for any offence, he is taken before a magistrate, who is seated at a table (as we see in the engraving.)   The prisoner is made to kneel in front of what forms the tribunal of

* The Rev   W   C   Milne's " Life in China."

justice—his captor on one side, and another policeman, with the instrument of punishment, on the other The magistrate has his clerk, but in no case is there either jury or pleading He hears the witnesses, and passes sentence, intimating the number of blows to be given (if flogging is awarded), by throwing on the ground some of the reeds which are seen in two small boxes at the corner of the table If it is an offence punishable by the bamboo, bastinado, or *cangue*, that punishment is immediately inflicted ; if it is more serious, and death or banishment is the sentence, the offender is sent to prison, or to the place of execution Persons charged with offences are seldom acquitted when there are no witnesses, the torture of the rack, &c, is frequently administered till the accused criminates himself

The prisoners condemned to death at Canton are executed without the gate, on the south side of the city, near the river. "When brought to the fatal spot," says a writer on Chinese punishments, "they kneel with their faces towards the emperor's court, and bending forward in the attitude of submission and reverence, suddenly expire beneath the bloody sword of the executioner." On this site, it is averred, that Yeh—the emperor's late commissioner at Canton, who was taken prisoner when that city was captured, and sent to Calcutta—had 70,000 Chinese put to death, some under circumstances of the most horrible cruelty, the description of which makes the blood run cold to read it.

There are four gaols in Canton, and they are generally full of prisoners The Chinese term for gaol is *te-yo*, or "earth's prison;" and most terrible prisons those of Canton were, and probably will be again, though they are improved for the present After the capture of that city in December, 1857, Lord Elgin, accompanied by the French commissioner, Baron Le Gros, inspected these prisons, it being reported that some Europeans were confined in them An eye-witness describes these places of confinement as "mere hovels, but within their yards," he says, "are beastly dens, 'stinking like monkey-houses,' closed with strong double gratings of the ubiquitous bamboo. From these dens, where the living had been lying among rotting corpses, were dragged forth and laid at the pitying feet of the commissioners, scores of miserable wretches, half-starved, covered with festering sores, lacerated from head to foot by torture and flagellation" Some of these wretched people had been bambooed on the feet till they could not walk, others were gashed about the abdomen and thighs, and some who had been bambooed that very morning, bleeding as they were, were in irons—their ankles being fettered together, and generally they had chains upon their wrists! It is said that 6,000 prisoners were confined in these prisons No Europeans were found, but it was ascertained that six—two Frenchmen, and four Englishmen—had died in prison not long previously. By Lord Elgin's orders, and in spite of the remonstrances of the Tartar general in command (who blustered, complained of being persecuted, and wanted to know what the Europeans had to do with his prisons), the poor maimed prisoners were removed to an hospital, and, whilst the English occupy Canton, they will not suffer such horrors to be repeated.

THE PUNISHMENT OF BAMBOOING.

"Flogging degrades, but it does not reform"

In China all petty offences are punished by flogging The instrument of punishment is formed from the stem of a gigantic grass or reed (common in the country), called the bamboo—one of the most useful products of the soil, being applied to a great variety of purposes *

No person in China, whatever his rank, is exempt from the punishment of flogging As we have stated elsewhere, officers of the army are subject to it A mandarin who interferes in government matters is fined, and receives besides eighty blows, as does any official who recommends an improper person for promotion, or is guilty of neglect or delay in performing the business of his office Subordinates of government are examined at the end of each year, and if they are found not to have improved, they receive forty blows. Physicians, who prescribe improperly for their patients, receive one hundred blows, the punishment of domestics for making a noise or disturbance in the imperial palace, is one hundred blows, and their masters (being considered responsible for the behaviour of their servants) receive fifty. The smallest number of blows inflicted is five The instrument with which they are administered is from four to five feet long, and two inches thick at the end that falls on the offender It is thinner at the end by which it is held, and the "great bamboo" weighs $2\frac{3}{4}$ lbs ; the lesser, 2 lbs. As soon as sentence is pronounced, the culprit is laid flat on his face, and receives his punishment—very often in the presence of his judge

Although no classes are exempt from this punishment, the rich have this advantage—that money will frequently purchase a mitigation of the sentence The police, who inflict the punishment, may, by the judicious application of a bribe, be induced to lay on fewer blows than are awarded, or to let them fall less heavily. So powerful is the effect of the bribe, that though the floggers are changed after every five or six strokes, lest the arm should become weak and the blows inefficient, yet they understand their business so well, that, notwithstanding the utmost care of the superintending mandarin, the flogging loses almost all its 'severity when the police have been feed There are also persons always to be found who will step into the prisoner's place, and become his substitute, for a "con-si-de-ra-ti-on," as Trapbois says Money, properly administered, will therefore frequently lead to the escape of the offender, the hired person being bambooed in his stead

When this punishment is administered with the vigour and strength which an able-bodied man can employ, the bamboo inflicts severe injury ; and, not unfrequently, death follows the flogging Under ordinary circumstances, as soon as the punishment is inflicted, the culprit must fall on his knees before the judge, and, bowing three times to the ground, return him humble thanks for the correction.

* See vol 1, p 22.

PUNISHMENT OF THE RACK.

" If you will
Add the corporeal rack, you may   these limbs
Will yield with age to crushing iron , but
There's that within my heart shall strain your engines "   BYRON.

ONE of the worst features in the criminal procedure of the Chinese is their retention of torture   While religious fanatics and hypocrites have been compelled to lay aside that horrible engine of barbarity, the rack, the Chinese are still permitted to employ it for the purpose of extorting confession; and, as Queen Victoria has interceded for the abolition of death as a punishment of apostasy in Turkey, it is to be hoped she will extend her humane influence to the extinction of an infinitely more cruel practice in China—a country which recent events have taught to respect her power

The Chinese rack is composed of a thick strong plank, having a contrivance at one end for securing the hands, and at the other a sort of double wooden vice   The vice is formed of three stout uprights, two of which are movable, but steadied by a block attached to each side   The ankles of the suspected culprit being placed in the machine, a cord is passed round the uprights, and held fast by two assistants, while the chief torturer gradually introduces a wedge into the intervals, alternately changing sides. This mode of forming an expansion at the upper part, causes the lower ends to draw towards the central upright, which is fixed into the plank, by which the ankles of the victim are painfully compressed, or completely crushed Should the unhappy sufferer be resolute from innocence, or obstinate from guilt, and submit to the consummation of the horrid procedure, his bones are ultimately reduced to a jelly.

Another mode of torture was witnessed by the Rev. W. Milne, at Ningpo. Opposite the mandarin's house, he saw a poor fellow kneeling on a coil of iron chains, his knees being bared, and his hands tied to a stake behind him, which two men held firmly in the ground   If he swerved to the right or left, a smart blow on the head from a whip brought him back to the right position   "The agonies of the poor fellow were evident from his quivering lips, pallid countenance, and tremulous voice, imploring relief, which was refused with the cold mocking command, ' Confess or suffer.' "

STREET PUNISHMENTS

"See—the officer of justice clears the way,
The prisoner passes, and the flagellator
His weapon brandishes, to execute the sentence"

The Chinese appear to be fond of public punishments; and we give two engravings, from Chinese drawings in the library of the East India Company, showing two culprits undergoing the sentences awarded by the mandarins. In our first plate there is a group of four figures, all engaged in receiving or administering a penalty awarded, we should say for piracy—when we look at the pigmy banners which are fixed behind the ears of the culprit, being apparently stuck into his head, causing a torture, we should think, at least equal to the flagellation itself. The first figure is striking a gong, this is to call the attention of the public, to whom he announces the crime, and the number of blows with the bamboo the prisoner is to receive. Then follows the prisoner, his hands tied behind him, and his countenance betraying both pain and terror, his feet are bare, and his dress of the thinnest description. The third figure is the flagellator, who brandishes the bamboos, four in number, as if he were intending to lay them on with a will. The fourth figure is a petty mandarin, who has the charge of the prisoner, and is present to see that the punishment is properly inflicted. The *ensemble* is indicative of an uncivilised and a barbarous *régime*, little accordant with European habits and modes of thinking in the nineteenth century.

In Plate II, the unhappy culprit is undergoing a species of torture. He is suspended from a cross-pole, supported by two uprights, by a rope passed round his neck and under his arms—his feet being tied together, and drawn up higher than the level of his head, by another. His breast rests on a long bamboo, which is held at each end by a policeman, and it is evident, that by elevating and lowering this pole, letting the prisoner fall upon it each time, the severity of the punishment is greatly increased.

The Chinese punishment of death is generally carried into effect by decapitating the culprit and that punishment is very dexterously performed. Mr. Meadows, the interpreter to the English embassy in China, was a witness, when at Canton in July, 1852, to the manner in which the Tartar officials beheaded some of the rebels (followers of Tai-ping), who fell into their power. The place of execution was a low room, entered by a strong iron-bound door. At one end was a species of shed, where the superintending mandarins sat, and before which a fire of fragrant sandal-wood was kept burning, to conceal the horrible effluvia arising from decomposed heads which had not been removed. Some of the prisoners walked in to this Golgotha, others were brought in in baskets, and tumbled out upon the floor, and there they lay motionless—the narrator could not tell whether from terror or previous punishment

A man stood behind each prisoner, and having placed him in a kneeling posture, he was compelled to put his head forward, his face inclining to the ground, his hands were placed behind his back, and grasped tightly by the attendant policeman He was made to keep this posture—which was a most painful one—till the executioner, with a sharp sword, struck off his head, which he did at one blow One man was crucified before he was beheaded He was bound to a wooden cross fixed against the wall, and the first horrible operation was to cut off the flesh from his forehead, breast, and extremities, with a short knife! When this was removed, he was taken down from the cross and instantly beheaded Such are the modes adopted by this "celestial people," as they term themselves, to punish those who offend against their laws

---

A CHINESE FIGARO.

"Early and late the busy streets he plies,
Startling the air anon with various cries
He shaves, the queue he dresses, and shampoos,
And whilst he s thus engaged, he tells the news"

THE barber is such an important agent in the Chinese social economy, that although we have already had something to say about him,* we are induced to return to the subject, giving the "Chinese Figaro" a plate to himself at the same time correcting a slight error in our former paper The barbers are not *all* itinerant There are, besides the locomotive pliers of the razor, the scissors, and the comb, "barbers in their own room, barbers with shops, and barbers who stand at the corner of the streets like Paris *commissionnaires*"† The total number of the "profession," in Canton alone, is said to be 20,000, and their shops in that city, are, what they formerly were in Europe, a place of meeting for idlers and scandal-mongers, it is there that tittle-tattle and ill-natured stories are bandied about, for China, too, has its slanderous chroniclers ‡

To *see* a Chinese barber perform his function of taking off a beard, for the first time, is enough to give an Englishman—accustomed as he is to the matchless razors with which the names of the Sheffield Rodgers and the metropolitan Mappin are identified—the horrors for the instrument used in China is a "wretched blade, two inches long and one broad, fitted into a piece of wood as a handle," and "resembling a clasp-knife, without a spring, broken in half" But, having *experienced* the operation, he is not afraid to undergo it again; for these Chinese knives are excellent substitutes for razors—they take off the beard completely and with ease, being scarcely felt when passing over the chin The Chinese barber has much to do besides shaving Having performed that operation in front, he goes to the queue

* See vol 1, pp 127, 128   † Dr. Yvan   ‡ *Ibid*

behind, which is first untied, then combed and plaited, next, any hairs that may have encroached upon the ears and nose are cleared away with pincers, and the aid of a little bamboo rod, tufted with soft carded cotton, is called into operation, and passed under the eyelids, all round the eye, and inside the ear, to brush off any dust or dirt, or loose hairs which may have lodged there. Nor is this all they examine the feet, and cut the nails and corns, if they require it; and then they shampoo their patient—an operation already described in our first volume.*

In China, the "barbers" only operate upon the males. The women have their hair dressed by their own sex—mothers, daughters, and sisters reciprocally performing the operation for each other, and the services of domestics and friends are occasionally called into requisition for the same purpose A Chinaman often, when he hears the twang of the barber's tweezers in the street, will send for him to perform his functions at his house, but he never approaches the interior apartments they are barred, and perhaps it is as well that they should be so.

Whenever it is practicable, the Chinese carry their burdens in a similar manner to that in which the barber conveys his utensils Fruits, vegetables, and all articles that can be placed in baskets, are divided, and with one basket at each end of the staff, men and women trudge along, the latter not shrinking from this drudgery When the load is too great for one man, it is swung from the middle of the staff, and carried by two, each taking one end on his shoulder—as we see our brewer's draymen convey casks of ale or porter from the dray to the publican's cellar The Coolies (or porters) find plenty of employment in China, parcels and luggage of every kind being conveyed in this manner. The constant action of the staff upon the shoulders of these Coolies hardens the skin, and it forms a sort of cushion on which the staff rests without causing irritation or pain, except in cases of excessive hard labour

---

FEMALE INDUSTRY IN CHINA.

"Cheerful she plies the needle and the thread,
And calm content beams in her open face."

In China, females are kept pretty much in the same seclusion that prevails in other parts of the East, but yet they are held in more respect there than some travellers are disposed to admit Although they have a maxim, that "a woman is thrice dependent before marriage, on her father, after marriage, on her husband; and when a widow, on her son"—still this dependence does not deprive them of the homage and respect of their sons, over whom they exercise at all times a species of authority Even the emperor performs the ceremonies of the *Koutou* before his mother, who is placed

* *Vide* vol 1, p 128

in a seat of honour to receive them In a Chinese house, the women's apartments constitute its sanctuary, but it is not so exclusive as in some Eastern countries When at Canton, Dr Yvan had free access to the women's quarter, in the house of Pan-se-Chen, his mandarin friend, and the particulars which he gives are not without interest He found much of splendour—little of comfort "The *petit* chamber of Madame Pan-se-Chen, for instance," he writes, "is an admirable boudoir—sofas, chairs, toilet-tables, and the rest, being made of beautiful wood, chiselled with infinite art; but her bed, lying underneath a network of gauze, is fitter for a nun's penance than to rest the soft limbs of a delicate lady A few strips of bamboo in a naukin palliasse, serve for a mattress, and the quilt is attached to a cotton sheet" Very delicate was the Chinese lady who inhabited these rooms, perhaps our readers will like to read the Doctor's description of her

"Madame Li, the legitimate wife of Pan-se-Chen, daughter of a powerful minister at the Court of Peking, was one of the most aristocratic beauties of the Flowery Land. This frail and delicate little creature resembled a sprig of jessamine, swayed by the wind, her loveable and tenderly-chiselled features wore an expression in which smiling and sadness were blended, one might have fancied her thoughts were rosy white, as the hue which art had lent to her cheeks Her eyes, like two black pearls, sent from behind the shelter of her silken lashes soft loquacious glances, or sparkling rays of innocent womanly malice Notwithstanding a little want of grace in its curve, her nose would not have disfigured a European countenance Madame Li was lady-like, after the manner of a charming young girl, her dignity was infantine in its grace And as on one of the great sofas of black wood, she sat see-sawing her legs backwards and forwards, showing her feet encased in slippers broidered with gold, and her ankles hung with bracelets, picking the leaves of an *eyulan* flower with her pretty little fingers, murmuring musically rather than talking, you would hardly help feeling as if you could eat her up like an orange flower."

This lady was in mourning, and was simply attired She appeared in a cham, or robe, of a very clear shade of blue, and wore an ornament, shaped like a comb, in her hair "but had she been got-up like a picture on rice-paper, she could not have been more charming." She was not the only occupant of the ladies' apartments There were twelve *tsié*, or concubines, who "represented all ages, all heights, and all degrees of plumpness" It was impossible to confound Madame Li with them "It was not that she had, in perfection, that air of imposing simplicity which bespeaks a woman of gentle blood, or that she was more elegantly dressed, but that she had the habit of command—a certain conscious superiority of carriage, sometimes breaking out into caprice, perhaps sometimes into anger, but which made you exclaim, 'This is the mistress here '"*

Music, painting, and embroidery, are the chief accomplishments of the Chinese ladies Their musical instruments are the harp, the lute, the guitar, they paint on silk and rice-paper, and embroider various articles for use and ornament, as is common in Europe The males have several appendages attached to a girdle fastened round their waist—such as a fan, usually contained in a worked silk sheath, a small bag, in which are deposited a flint and steel for lighting the inevitable pipe, a purse, and a watch-case these articles are usually the work of the ladies, and display

* "Inside of Canton "

their talents in embroidery and design   The females of a lower class pursue industrial employments as the means of subsistence   The handsome crape shawls brought to England from China, are the work of women, and spinning, weaving, and sewing, are the daily occupations of the wives and daughters of the humbler classes

In the mountains of China, where the habits of the females are still extremely simple, and where they are very industrious, they use the distaff in spinning—a neat and simple piece of machinery, with a broad wheel, not unlike the wool-wheels in use in England not so many years ago   Amongst the Chinese paintings in the library of the East India Company, is one representing a Chinese female and her mother, the former with a distaff by her side, and a wicker-basket—in which the skeins of thread or cotton were placed, at the close of each day's work—for her seat   Her mother holds a piece of cloth in her hand, which she is evidently showing to a man, who, armed with a spear, and with a bow and quiver at his back, occupies the foreground   this man holds a bundle of cloth under his arm, which he has, no doubt, just purchased of the fair vendors   Another picture shows us a female in her loom, weaving, the machine bearing a great resemblance to the looms of this country, indeed, the principle is precisely the same.   Except for the features of the industrious occupant of the loom, which are decidedly Chinese, the device might be taken for a scene in an English cottage years ago, when hand-loom weaving was a common occupation   A *petit* plate with cakes, a teapot, and cup and saucer, are also by the side of the loom, denoting the refreshment of which its fair occupant had been partaking, or was about to partake   Close by those articles is a small taper, in a candlestick like those used by our working classes   It is burning, and denotes the time to be night   The Chinese weavers, we are told, work many hours—quite as many as those in this country are obliged to devote to their labour and toil

The Chinese silk and cotton manufactures are all produced in hand-looms, and mostly by women   There are few large manufacturing establishments, but the artizans work on their own account, and they quite compete with European skill and capital so far as cheapness of production is concerned   In quality, the Chinese textile manufactures are equal to our own

Our engraving represents a female sempstress   She is making stockings from a material for which others of her sex have spun the thread and wove the cloth, and very happy she looks at her work.   Her materials are very much like what are used by sempstresses in this country; and her costume is the ordinary one of the Chinese female, whose dresses are all made high up to the neck, as shown in the picture

CLEANING COTTON.

"How generally the cotton-plant is grown,
In countries wide apart its use is known
Thousands by it obtain the means to live,
To young and old it num'rous comforts give."

WE have already noticed the growth and manufacture of cotton in China * our engraving represents an early stage of the latter—the cleaning the cotton-wool, before it passes into the hands of the spinner As soon as the husbandman in China has got in his harvest—frequently on the very day that he concludes it,—he sows the seed of the cotton-plant He does this by removing some of the soil with an iron rake, scattering the seed, and then raking the earth over it again. It requires a fall of rain, or dew, to moisten it; it then makes its appearance above ground, shooting up gradually till it attains a height of about two feet The flowers, commonly of a yellow colour, but sometimes nearly red, appear in August. They are succeeded by pods about the size of a nut, which, opening in three places, about forty days after the first appearance of the flower, discovers in each three or four bags of cotton, exceedingly white, and of the same form as the coil of a silkworm. To the fibres of the cotton are fastened the seeds which are to be sown the next season, and they are separated from the fibre by the following process —A machine is prepared consisting of two cylinders, about a foot long and an inch thick, one of wood, the other of iron, or both of wood These are so near together that nothing can pass between but the cotton Being put in motion by means of a foot-wheel, the pods are applied on one side, and the revolution of the cylinders draws in the cotton-wool, which is ejected on the opposite side, while the seeds are struck off, and fall into a receptacle placed underneath The cotton-wool thus separated from the seed, has to be freed by another process from the knots and dirt which may have accumulated For this purpose, a very elastic bow, with a tight spring, is held by the workman in his left hand, over a heap of cotton-wool The bow is connected with another string fastened to a bamboo, which is attached to a belt at the back of the man, and passes over his head in a curve Pulling down the string with some force, over a heap of the cotton-wool, by means of a wooden instrument held in his right hand, he suddenly makes the bow recoil The vibration thus occasioned is kept up till the heap of wool is entirely scattered and loosened, and separated into fine white flocks, without breaking or otherwise injuring the fibre It then passes to the spinner

The manufacture of cotton has been known in all ages of the Chinese empire Marco Polo mentions the Nanking cottons, and their various-coloured threads—each colour being imparted by nature, and not the consequence of a dye In one

* See vol i, pp 155—157

of their great works on agriculture, the most minute directions are given for the culture of the cotton-plant, according to the different varieties of soil, climate, &c , and they seem judicious and appropriate   " With the national disposition to make the most of everything, the Chinese, besides manufacturing the cotton produced, express an oil from the seed, and, when the oil is expressed, use the seeds for manure the capsules or pods being hard and woody, they burn as firewood, and the leaves they give to their cattle; 'so that,' as the author of the before-mentioned agricultural work observes, 'every part of the vegetable is appropriated to some useful object '"*

The cotton manufacture is still one of great importance in China, and the East generally, but not so much so as it was before the inventions of Hawkins, Arkwright, Crompton, Cartwright, and others—aided by the application of steam to manufacturing purposes—enabled the English manufacturer to compete with, and finally to rise superior to, those of China and Hindostan, who had, long before attention was devoted to the production of cotton fabrics in this country, "arrived at such perfection in the arts of spinning and weaving, that the lightness and delicacy of their finest cloths emulated the web of the gossamer, and seemed to set competition at defiance " Now we supply both China and Hindostan, to a certain extent , and although scarcely three-quarters of a century has elapsed since the British cotton manufacture was in its infancy, it has become, next to agriculture, that which employs the greatest number of hands, in which the largest amount of capital has been invested, and which stands highest in the value both of the domestic consumption and foreign exports.

* Oliphant's " China "

THE

OVERLAND ROUTE TO CHINA AND INDIA.

***

" Mother of wealth, and enterprise, and arts
Her golden empire marries distant parts,
She knits the league, she sheathes the blade of war,
Of earth and sea, and man the conqueror
Dread agent or for boundless good or ill,
God speaks the word, and *Commerce* works his will "   C J C

As the intercourse between England and India increased—as the trade between the two countries augmented, and the benefits of lawful commerce flowed from the conquests our arms had made—and as a knowledge of the countries which laid between our island home and her empire in the East became better diffused, the attention of many who were interested in the connection between the two quarters of the globe, became directed to the questions—whether there were not means for shortening the route, and for reducing the time necessary for the voyage from one to the other ? One of the first persons who succeeded in bringing speculation upon this point to a practical issue, was the late Lieutenant Waghorn   This officer was born at Chatham in 1800   He entered the navy at an early age , and after performing his duty zealously for some years, by sea and land, and having obtained a respite from active service, he turned his attention to the establishment of a steam communication between England and India   Subsequently he projected the overland route   Having laid his plans before the Court of Directors, they sent him, in 1829, to India, by way of Egypt   He traversed the continent to Trieste, which port he reached in nine days and a-half   He was twenty-six days before he arrived at Alexandria, from whence he went to Cairo, and crossed the desert to Suez   Here he expected to find a steam-vessel, but being disappointed, he took an open boat, and went down the Red Sea, to Jeddah—a voyage which occupied six days and a-half, being a distance of 620 miles   Again disappointed of a steamer, he returned to Suez, quite convinced that the route he had traversed was that which ought, from every reason—moral, political, and commercial—to be adopted   He reduced his plan into form, and advocated it publicly, and though he met with much praise, finding few inclined to give him active assistance, he set about himself, opening out the overland route   In the course of 1830 and 1831, he laid down the route across the desert   Making Alexandria his starting-place he passed from there to Cairo, and established eight halting-posts between that town and Suez, put carriages on the road, and himself worked the overland mail from 1831 to 1836   In February of the latter year, he carried letters from Bombay to England in forty-seven days   Nine years later—on the 30th of October, 1845—he arrived in London from Bombay, which he left on the 1st, and he projected a still shorter route, by which he calculated he should reduce the journey and voyage between Bombay and London to twenty-one days   He was never, however, supported as his zeal and public spirit deserved, and he died in 1850, having exhausted all his pecuniary means in carrying out his great enterprise   Since that period, the "Overland Route" has fallen into the hands of the Peninsular and Oriental Steam Navigation Company, which has now a navy of about fifty five steamers, employs, afloat and ashore, above 4,000 persons, pays upwards of £100,000 per annum in salaries, and as much for coals   Yet large profits are made—a proof of the magnitude of the traffic

The intercourse with China, as well as that to India, is carried on now by the Overland Route ; and that is our reason for introducing a description of that route into our Sketches of the Celestial Empire

The steamers of the Peninsular and Oriental Company start from Southampton.   Sometimes passengers go by London, Dover, Calais, Paris, and Marseilles, where they take a steamer to Malta, and from thence to Alexandria   But the most common route is to take the steamer at Southampton —a seaport standing on a peninsula jutting out between the mouths of the Test and Itchin rivers, at the head of Southampton Water, the name of a beautiful and picturesque bay, an inlet from the English Channel   This port has not much foreign, and only a limited coasting trade , but since it has become the station for the West India, Mediterranean, East India, and China mails, its importance has greatly increased, and it has now communication by rail with the metropolis (from which it is eighty miles distant), and all the principal towns in England , and by steamers, with the ports on the south coast, Ireland, and the Channel Islands.   The views in the neighbourhood of Southampton are among the most attractive in England, and the High-street is adorned with noble buildings, which render its appearance very imposing

To those wh   en j   a r   u   m   " is   int r   ng   When the steamer leaves th   t   t   W   t   n l   ntr   ln   t   n t Osborne, is distinctly seen in   s an   C   f   m tt   fr t   u r of ships and yachts that anchor there, and when those are passed, the Needles come in sight—those "singular rocks," observes a voyager, "so singularly named, standing erect among the billows, as the body-guard of this, the Queen of all England's lovely isles, of which they, at one time, no doubt, formed a part." After the shores of England are left behind in the distance, Ushant is seen, and soon the English Channel is left, and the Bay of Biscay (in which the swelling surge always predominates) entered. Here navigation is greatly impeded by the north-west wind, and by what is called "Rennell's Current," which sets in from the Atlantic, and sweeps round the north coast of Spain. Breasting the current, the steamer passes Cape Ortegal, and keeps off the Spanish coast, steering to the southward. One traveller, describing the route, says, "We passed near Corunna's lone shore,—bold, bleak, desolate. Fires blazing on the hills, and in the valleys between—the people making charcoal—had a striking effect, as seen from the deck of the steamer." Passing Cape Finisterre, the west of Portugal is skirted, and in fine weather, Oporto, Torres Vedras, and Ciudad, are seen in the distance. Arriving off Cape St Vincent, the Gulf of Cadiz is crossed, Cape Trafalgar reached, and shortly after the steamer passes the town of Tarifa, standing on the extreme southern point of Spain and of Europe, fifteen miles south-west of Gibraltar, and defended by an old castle, built by the Moors under whom it was a military fort of importance, as it is now to the Spaniards.

Gibraltar is reached in five days from Southampton, and it is the first place where the steamer stops to take in coals—anchoring under the far-famed rock. The approach to it, by the straits, opens out, in fine weather, magnificent scenery. The Straits of Gibraltar are fifteen miles long, and about seven broad. On one side is Mount Abile, on the other, Calpe, or "the Rock of Gibraltar"—two proud eminences, once united, as classic legends tell, till Hercules cleft them asunder, to open a passage between the Mediterranean Sea and the Atlantic Ocean, and even to this day, they are called the "Pillars of Hercules." Calpe (from Calph, which, in the ancient Phœnician tongue, signified a "carved mountain") is a promontory about three miles long, from north to south, and from half to three-quarters of a mile across, from east to west. An isthmus of sand connects it with the continent, the rock itself being composed of grey limestone or marble, and containing numerous caves. This rock rises nearly 1,500 feet above the sea, on every side except the west, which shelves down to the bay, and on that side the town is built. It consists merely of two or three long streets, running parallel with the sea-wall, and these streets are intersected by narrow lanes, conveyed up the side of the rock by steps—which are very unpleasant to climb on a hot day. The town was originally founded by a Moor, named Tarik or Tarif, hence its name, Gib-el-Tarik, "Mountain of Tarik." It is defended on all sides where access is possible, and constitutes one of the strongest, but not the strongest, fortress in the world.

Leaving Gibraltar, and entering upon the Mediterranean Sea, the voyagers have, on their left, the Spanish town of Algesiras, and the mountains of the Sierra Nevada, whose lofty peaks—12,800 feet high—are always covered with snow, and, on their right, the town of Algiers. The steamer generally skirts the African coast, leaving the islands of Sardinia and Sicily considerably on the left, and is, not unfrequently, visited by the native African craft, bringing fruit and vegetables, so delicious at all times when received fresh from the gardens, and more especially so at sea. Two islands of considerable interest—Pantelaria and Galeta—are passed, as are the ruins of old Carthage, and here "the scene is often pleasantly enlivened by numerous small Sicilian and other vessels, that cross from different parts of Italy to the coast of Barbary, Malta, &c." That island is the next station of the steamer, which stops there to take in passengers, mails, and coal. The voyage from Gibraltar to Malta occupies five days.

Malta is one of a group of three islands—the others being Gozo and Comino, the former being about five miles north-west of Malta, and the latter lying in the channel, called the Straits of Fregia, which runs between them. Malta—seventeen miles long, nine wide, where it is the farthest across, and about fifty in circumference—lies further from the mainland than any island in the Mediterranean. Its position renders its possession a desideratum to any power which has connections in that sea, and it has successively belonged to the Phœnicians, the Greeks, the Carthaginians, the Romans, the Arabs, the Norman rulers of Sicily, Germany, the Knights of St John, the Turks, the French, and the English, who have held it since 1800. Gozo and Comino are considered as dependencies of Malta. The inhabitants of the three islands are a mixed race. The Roman Catholic religion prevails amongst them, and they are by no means an enlightened or intelligent people, though great improvement has been manifested since the English occupation. La Valetta is the capital of Malta—a handsome town on the north-east coast built upon a tongue of land which projects into the bay, and has, from the curving of the coast, an excellent harbour on both sides, these harbours generally present the most animated appearance. Many vessels float on the waters, and steamers are constantly seen leaving them. Above them rise rocks covered with almost every species of fortification, and buildings of all kinds. The south, or great harbour of Valetta, is defended by three forts—St Elmo, Ricasoli, and St Angelo, beyond them lies the chief suburb of the capital, Vittoriosa, which is also strongly fortified. Valetta—founded by the grand-master, Valetta, in 1566—has a fine appearance from the sea. It stands on very uneven ground, many of the streets being successive flights of steps, but it is clean, and has several noble buildings. The principal one is the residence of the governor, formerly that of the grand master of the Knights of St John, when the island was in their possession. The English collegiate church, built by Queen Adelaide, at an expense of £15,000, and the library, with its 60,000 volumes, also deserve attention. The capital boasts of its university and royal dockyard, it is the residence of the governor, the seat of all the principal authorities, and the centre of the commerce of the island. Besides Valetta, there is another fortified city in Malta—Citta Vecchia, or Notabile. It stands on a limestone hill in which are catacombs. It has a suburb called Rabato on the south-west s... in which a ... the apostle Paul, and, on a north coast, to the westward of Valetta, is a ... called Porto de San Paulo or Port of St Paul. Malta being supposed to be the Melita mentioned in ... that spot the ... of St Paul's shipwreck.

The population of Malta is enormous—about 105,000, or 1,100 to the square mile. Gozo which is more carefully cultivated than Malta, has a richer soil, and supplies the larger island with much of its food, has 16,000 inhabitants. There are several churches and convents on that island, and also many natural curiosities, which, with the ruins scattered in all directions, are worth visiting. One of these, "The Giant's Tower," is a very remarkable object. According to tradition, it is the work of the Cyclops, whose abode was on Mount Etna, and, composed as it is of "enormous masses of unhewn rock, piled one on another, without mortar or cement," we may well wonder how it could be constructed. Apart from the legend, it is thought that this remarkable edifice " was a 'paratheion'—a temple of fire-worshippers, and it is supposed to be a monument of the skill and mechanical power of the Phœnicians the aboriginal inhabitants of the island "* Comino is merely an islet with 900 inhabitants. It is defended by a fort, which Wignacourt, a grand-master, erected in 1618. There are no other buildings on the island except the few huts in which the peasants reside.

But we must not dwell any longer on Malta, for the steamer is leaving for Alexandria, which it reaches in three days. There is nothing beyond the usual routine of a sea voyage to notice on the route, and when the coast of Egypt is first discovered, it has an arid and barren appearance, which soon wears off, and changes to one of great animation. As the steamer approaches Alexandria, various objects on shore—the fort, the palace of the pasha, the lighthouse, called Farillon, which occupies the site where the far-famed Pharos once stood—attract notice, and it is seldom but that the harbour is full of vessels. The pasha's fleet lies there, and when the steamer arrives at night, and by moonlight, the effect is very beautiful. Alexandria derives its name from its founder, Alexander the Great. It is now, as it was in ancient times, the principal seaport of Egypt, having between 60,000 and 70,000 inhabitants, who carry on a considerable commerce both with the East and West. In ancient times, according to the descriptions left us by Strabo and other writers, Alexandria was a most magnificent city, its principal street (2,000 feet in length) being covered with splendid edifices. It was also the scene of many interesting events—the translation of the Old Testament into the Greek version, called the Septuagint, and the preaching of the Gospel by St Mark, being two of greatest interest—and the depository of two of the most famous libraries ever collected. The first, of 40,000 volumes, was accidentally burnt when Cæsar took the city, 47 B C, the second which comprised 700,000 volumes, was wantonly destroyed by the Saracens, under the Caliph Omar, A D. 642, by whose command the baths of the place were heated for six months with books instead of wood.

The ancient city was on the mainland, the modern city (which has 60,000 inhabitants) stands on a peninsula (the ancient island of Pharos), and on the isthmus that connects it with the continent. Of its general aspect—

" The most that can be said is, that it is an inferior continental town, its streets peopled with Englishmen, Italians, and Greeks, whose wives dress in bonnets and Paris mantles, and go out shopping in the afternoon, in one-horse clarences and pony-phaetons. Mosques there are, it is true, but, being in the back streets, they are unseen, except by the curious in such matters, there are also bazaars but they are far from picturesque, and decidedly dirty. As to turbans, there is a tendency in the people to wind cloths round their heads but it is a hard run between them and the wearers of hats. There are a great many camels, but no trees, except palms, no shrubs, but prickly pears, and no plants, but orange-trees and bananas. On the whole, Alexandria appears eastern only in name, position on the map, and from the fact of its possessing Cleopatra's Needles and Pompey's Pillar "†

The former are not far from the ruins of Cleopatra's palace, which was built on the walls facing the port. They are of Thebal stone, sixty feet high by seven feet square, and covered with hieroglyphics. One is standing upright on its pedestal, the other has been, for many years, lying on the strand. It has been presented to the British government, but the expense and risk of its removal have hitherto prevented its transfer to England. Pompey's Pillar, ninety-four feet high, stands at the distance of nearly a mile from the city, on the road to the Lake Mareotis.

Till recently, passengers to India or China travelled from Alexandria to Cairo by the Mahmoudie canal, being landed at Boulac, the port of the Egyptian capital, two miles from the city, to which they were conveyed in omnibuses. It was evening or night when they arrived at Boulac, where great confusion always prevailed while their luggage was weighed and assorted—all the heavy portion being forwarded to Suez, and only common necessaries and light packages retained. The confusion was caused by the assemblage of dragomen, porters, donkey-boys, torch-bearers, hotel-keepers, and vau-drivers, all anxious for customers, by them and their camels, horses, and dogs, a perfect Babel was created. Once in the omnibus, the passengers started immediately, with torch-bearers running on each side of the vehicle, passing through a broad but winding and dusty road, flanked by " high walls, huge cactuses, and noble trees," to the capital, where, admission being obtained, the British hotel was the destination of most of the English. The first vans for crossing the desert usually started early the next morning, others followed at stated times, but as they were all numbered, and the passengers drew lots for them before they reached Alexandria, they had no choice of time, and many of them had no opportunity of seeing anything of the city.

Cairo, or Grand Cairo, as it is frequently called (the El Masr, "the capital" of the Egyptians, and El Kahirah, " the victorious," of the Arabs) is seated near the right bank of the Nile, five miles from the origin of the Delta, occupying a favourable site upon a plain at the foot of the mountain-chain called Jebel Makkatan It was founded by Jawhar, a Moggrebin general, in the middle of the tenth century, and soon became the residence of the Arab rulers, as it now is of the Turkish pasha, formerly only the viceroy of the sultan, but the office, since 1840, has been hereditary in the family of Mehemet Ali. Its population is estimated at between 250,000 and 300,000, and it is divided into the old and the new cities, which are separated by a series of gardens and plantations. Old Cairo consists of a suburb called Misr-el-Aatik, by the Arabs, and Fostat, by others, and, with B . . . .   except seven

* " Overla . . . . L. .   in the L . . . .d   † L . . . ra & t . . .   . . . Kennard

towers, called the Granaries of Joseph, which are still used to store corn, and a pretty church, frequented alike by the Christians and Copts—the descendants of the aboriginal inhabitants of the country A well, called Joseph's Well, is also in the vicinity. New Cairo has an imposing appearance It is divided into the Coptic, the Jew, and the Frank quarters, which are separated by gates, is traversed by a canal of irrigation, beginning at Old Cairo, and surrounded by a battlemented wall, with towers at every hundred paces The streets are narrow and unpaved, each being closed by a gate, the most beautiful houses are built on the banks of the canal, those in the other parts of the city being gloomy, and not distinguished for comfort There are some fine mosques, the largest—that of Azbar—being in the centre of the city, and the citadel, which appears to spring from the midst of a grove of fine lofty trees, is a conspicuous object Outside the walls are the palace of the pasha, originally built by Saladin, in the twelfth century—the tombs of the Mamelukes, and the Obelisk of Heliopolis —all worth visiting About seven miles from the opposite banks of the Nile, are the Pyramids, which most travellers endeavour to visit

The vans which, under the old system, conveyed the passengers across the desert, would seat six persons, tightly packed They were dispatched at intervals, four or six starting at one time, the total number being regulated by that of the passengers There was always an interval of two or three hours between each dispatch They started according to their numbers, and the passengers took their places according to the lots previously drawn • The journey was a dreary one, little meeting the eye but a wide and apparently boundless tract of arid sand, and the numerous bodies of dead camels, that were seen in every direction Occasionally, an Arab horseman was met, or a camel with his solitary rider Less frequently, caravans of merchants, or of pilgrims, would cross the traveller's path, and nearly in the centre of the desert, stands a solitary acacia tree, called "the mother of rags," because the pilgrims rest under it when returning from Mecca, and before they start again, each attaches to it a piece of cloth or cotton, linen or silk, torn from his clothes There were fourteen stations between Cairo and Suez They were as well conducted as it was possible for them to be The central one had many of the comforts of an English hotel, and the proprietors, or keepers, were respectable men At all, the travellers had the means of ablution provided, and they could stretch their limbs for an hour upon the sofas, with which they were plentifully furnished In starting from these stations, there was always a struggle between the drivers of the vans for the first place, and the equerry, who was appointed by the pasha to take charge of the expedition, mounted on a beautiful and spirited Arabian horse, had frequently great difficulty in keeping order This journey, from Cairo to Suez, was frequently performed in eighteen hours

The journey from Alexandria to Cairo, 130 miles and from Cairo to Suez, 90 miles, is now performed by rail, the passengers being conveyed in omnibuses from the hotel to the station, the whole journey being completed in less time than that from Suez used to be, and, of course, is much less fatiguing to the passengers The railway is the sole property of his highness the Pasha of Egypt The rails are laid on iron sleepers The work was executed under the superintendence of Robert Stephenson, Esq, M P, and the engineers, drivers, and carriages are all English

The town of Suez is situated near the head of the gulf of that name, the western arm of the Red Sea It is built on a low, sandy tract of land, the country around it is desert, and provisions and water have to be brought from Sinai and Egypt The streets are not paved, and the houses are built of sun-dried brick There are about a dozen mosques, a Greek church, a custom-house, and other public buildings, 500 houses, and about 5,000 inhabitants, but it presents a miserable ensemble, from the absence of all verdure and vegetation It is a station, however, for numerous caravans and travellers Vessels of more than sixty tons cannot enter the harbour The steamers are moored two miles from the town, and the passengers and luggage are conveyed to them in native craft

The view, on steaming from Suez, is picturesque Insted of the desert which has just been quitted, Mount Sinai is seen, attractive in itself, and much more so from the holy associations connected with it Other hills and mountains are also seen on the Arabian shore The Gulf of Suez is twenty-eight miles in length, and ridges of table-land rise on both sides, to the height of near 3,000 feet It terminates at the extremity of the peninsula of Sinai, where the Gulf of Akabah joins it, and from thence to the Straits of Bab-el-Mandeb, the united mass of waters is called the Red Sea, or Sea of Edom This sea, 1,280 miles long, 200 miles broad, having a depth of 400 feet, and containing 890,000 cubic miles, receives no river, and is covered with sunken rocks, sand-banks, and small islands, rendering the navigation very intricate and dangerous Many of the rocks are coral reefs, and from those reefs, or from the blood-red hue frequently imparted to the waters by animalculæ, the name is supposed to have been derived The principal chain of mountains in Arabia runs nearly parallel with the east shore, and they increase in elevation as they extend inland From the decks of the passing vessels, this ever-changing mountain scenery is very grand, but nothing can be more desolate and dreary than the shore itself The monsoons continually prevail in this sea, the south-west monsoon for eight months, and the north west for four The heat is intense, and the passage from Suez to Aden, which occupies eight days, is the most trying to the passengers, and deaths are not unfrequent In the 1,300 miles, very few towns are seen Thubare and El Wursh are two small harbours at the upper part of the sea, on the Arabian coast, beyond which the mountains rise in lofty magnificence Native vessels, conveying goods, and others with fishermen, are seen off the ports On the African side is Cosseir, where passengers are taken up, and lower down, on the Asiatic bank, Jeddah, where the pilgrims disembark, on their way to Mecca and Medina—a place rendered notorious by the wanton massacre of the French consul there, with other Europeans, in 1858, for which a speedy vengeance was taken by Captain Pullen in her majesty's frigate Cyclops As the steamer nears the Straits of Bab-el-Mandeb, the town of Mocha, famous for its coffee, can be distinctly seen

The Straits of Bab-el-Mandeb which unite the Red Sea with the Indian Ocean, are about twenty miles across. The coast is formed by the Peak of Bab-el-Mandeb (the south-west extremity of Arabia), to the east.

Ingram Content Group UK Ltd.
Milton Keynes UK
UKHW052159090323
418230UK00018B/770